GLOBAL ORGANIZATIONS

The Caribbean Community

GLOBAL ORGANIZATIONS

The African Union

The Arab League

The Association of Southeast Asian Nations

The Caribbean Community

The European Union

The International Atomic Energy Agency

The Organization of American States

The Organization of the Petroleum
Exporting Countries

The United Nations

The United Nations Children's Fund

The World Bank and
the International Monetary Fund

The World Health Organization

The World Trade Organization

GLOBAL ORGANIZATIONS

The Caribbean Community

Brenda Lange

Series Editor
Peggy Kahn
University of Michigan–Flint

CHELSEA HOUSE PUBLISHERS
An imprint of Infobase Publishing

The Caribbean Community

Chelsea House
An imprint of Infobase Publishing
132 West 31st Street
New York NY 10001

Library of Congress Cataloging-in-Publication Data
Lange, Brenda.
  The Caribbean Community / by Brenda Lange.
     p. cm. — (Global organizations)
  Includes bibliographical references and index.
  ISBN 978-0-7910-9541-6 (hardcover)
 1. Caribbean Community. 2. Caribbean Area—Economic conditions.
3. Caribbean Area—Politics and government. 4. Caribbean Area—Social
conditions. I. Title.
  HC151.L36 2009
  337.1'729—dc22   2008055363

CONTENTS

Where Is
the Caribbean?

THE CARIBBEAN COMMUNITY, OR CARICOM, WAS FORMALLY established on July 4, 1973, with the signing of the Treaty of Chaguaramas. That date was chosen to honor the birthday of one of Jamaica's national heroes—Norman Washington Manley. Manley was an advocate of the West Indies Federation, the original attempt to integrate countries in the Caribbean Basin. The signing of the Treaty of Chaguaramas was the end result of a nearly two-decade-long effort to unify these countries and cement bonds between them. The goal of the community is to build cooperation among the member states in order to improve the Caribbean economies and the general well-being of the populations. CARICOM is an organization of many, but not all, of the island countries in the Caribbean Basin.

CARIBBEAN GEOGRAPHY

The Caribbean is a distinct region that has lured people to its shores from the time it was first discovered by outsiders. The area is made up of more than 7,000 islands, islets, reefs, and cays (pronounced keys) in an archipelago (or chain of islands) surrounding the Caribbean Sea. The Caribbean Sea is one of the world's largest saltwater seas, covering an area of more than one million miles. It has little exchange of deep water with the Atlantic Ocean and is mostly enclosed by the islands and coastlines. In addition to the 7,000 named and unnamed landforms, the coastlines of Central America and South America also are considered part of the Caribbean Basin. The basin is located southeast of the Gulf of Mexico and the Florida Keys, north of South America, and east of Mexico and Central America.

The islands are divided into three groups: the Greater Antilles, the Lesser Antilles, and the Bahamas. Spain, France, and England all fought over these islands for their natural resources. The islands also provided perfect landing points for the ships that traveled regularly back and forth between Europe and the New World.

The Greater Antilles includes Cuba, Jamaica, Puerto Rico, Hispaniola (which encompass Haiti and the Dominican Republic), and the Cayman Islands. The Lesser Antilles— Barbados, St. Kitts, Antigua, Martinique, and Guadeloupe— form an arc on the easternmost edge of the Caribbean Sea and are part of a volcanic archipelago. The curve begins in the north near Puerto Rico, bends inward along the northern coast of Venezuela, and is comprised of about three dozen islands and cays. The islands of the Greater and Lesser Antilles are considered part of North America and are joined by the islands of the Bahamas (another archipelago of 700 islands and 2,000 cays). Columbus's first landfall was in this area on an island he named San Salvador.

The islands are concentrated in a relatively small area, yet their climate and geography are varied. Some are mountainous, while others are relatively flat. The overall climate is tropical,

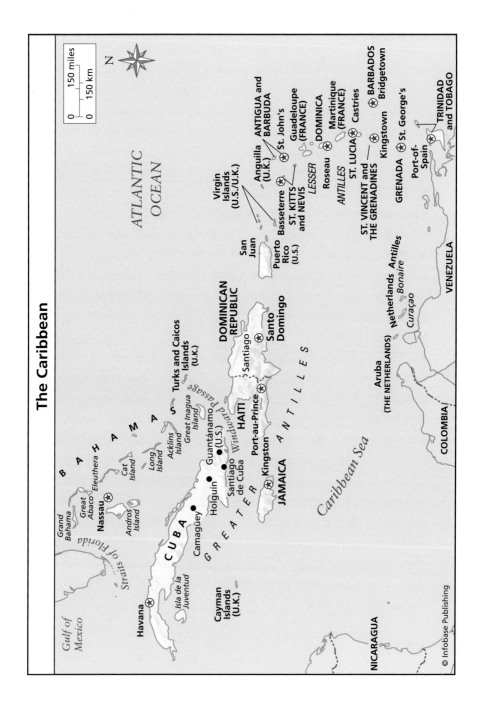

The Caribbean

© Infobase Publishing

but some islands are partially arid, and rainfall amounts vary with elevation. Some resemble rainforests on one side and deserts on another. A wide range of plant and animal life is supported in this great, diverse region. Because so many of them face environmental threats, the Caribbean Islands have been named a "biodiversity hotspot" by Conservation International. A biodiversity hotspot is an area in which natural ecosystems are relatively intact but the species of animals, rainforests, and reefs within them are threatened. Sea life, including hundreds of varieties of fish and coral reefs, is especially endangered.

EARLY HISTORY OF THE CARIBBEAN

Centuries ago the Carib and Arawak Indians lived on the Caribbean Islands. Before them were the Ciboneys, who came to the Caribbean about four or five thousand years ago but had already been driven to Cuba and Haiti by the Arawak. They were extinct within a century after European contact. The Arawak, also known as Taino (which means "peace"), lived on what are today Cuba, Jamaica, Haiti, and the Dominican Republic. Society was organized around their religion, with a large group of gods known as *zemis,* represented by symbols of wood, stone, and bones. The people fed their zemis and gave them tobacco to make them happy so they would protect them from diseases and hurricanes.

The Caribs lived on the island chain to the east, including St. Lucia, St. Vincent, and Trinidad, and are believed to have

(*Opposite page*) The Caribbean Islands comprise more than 7,000 islands, islets, reefs, and cays. This region is also called the West Indies, because when Christopher Columbus arrived in 1492 he believed he had reached India. Due to its colonial history, the West Indies is a region of ministates and the population, estimated at 34.5 million, is multiracial and multicultural.

come from the rainforests of Venezuela in South America. They seemed to live more simply, although their artifacts are similar to those found on islands populated by the Arawak. Both groups were tropical forest people who fished, hunted, and traveled from island to island by canoe. The Caribs were believed to be the more warlike of the two tribes, raiding other tribes to bring home wives for the young men. They wore their dark hair oiled and long, and their native dress consisted of parrot feathers, necklaces made of victims' teeth, and red body paint.[1]

The Indians' simple way of life was shattered with the arrival of the first Europeans. Christopher Columbus and his crew first spotted the islands in 1492. Believing he had reached India, Columbus named the islands the West Indies. Estimates vary about the number of indigenous peoples who lived among these islands before Columbus's arrival. Some anthropologists estimate several million; others believe it was somewhere around three-quarters of a million.

The Spanish and Portuguese led the influx of Europeans. Over the next century they were joined by the British, the French, and the Dutch. Many Indians died from malaria, which is a disease common in tropical climates, and smallpox, which was brought to the islands by the Europeans.

The peaceful Arawaks were more easily dominated by the invaders, but the tougher, warlike Caribs resisted European settlements on Dominica and St. Vincent. The Caribs destroyed the first English colony on St. Lucia in 1641. Eventually most were killed in battle, assimilated during colonialism, or retained areas such as Dominica. Much of the natives' indigenous culture died along with them, although some of their traditions and foods such as nuts, pineapples, maize, cashews, and tobacco are now known worldwide.

The Europeans came for financial gain—to take riches back to their homeland. They never intended to integrate themselves into the existing society, but wanted to conquer and control. They believed they were justified in taking over the islands, since they considered themselves racially superior. Settlers came in increasing numbers, trying to recreate the societies from which they came and restructuring the Indians' social, political, and religious lives.

The settlers nearly wiped out the indigenous peoples. Many of the survivors were forced into slavery, setting up an early caste system with the white settler at the top. The unique labor force of the islands came to be comprised of settlers, African slaves, Asians, and the few remaining Indians. The region was developed unevenly as first one country landed and settled an island, then was challenged by another. The skirmishes left the region in upheaval and confused the natives, who had trouble keeping track of who was in charge. The settlers—the British, Spanish, French, Danish, Dutch, Portuguese, and Swedish—imported their own culture and traditions and established their own form of local government. And *everything* was made more difficult by the pirates who freely roamed the Caribbean Sea until the end of the seventeenth century.

Tobacco and cotton were grown at first, but the introduction and success of sugar plantations made it necessary to find many more workers to plant and harvest the demanding sugar crop. The answer came in the form of slaves brought from central and western Africa. Thousands of slaves were brought to the Caribbean under harrowing conditions, with slaves far outnumbering the white settlers. Although the slave trade was abolished in several countries in the early nineteenth century, illegal slavery continued until the 1870s.[2] In response, indentured servants were brought from India, China, and the East Indies. The people who today are regarded as native to the islands are mostly descendents of African slaves, their European masters, and these indentured Asians.

THE TRANSATLANTIC SLAVE TRADE

The Caribbean was at the center of the transatlantic slave trade, as European settlers devised a powerful and brutal system to make money from sugar and other crops. Advances in science—maps, compasses, and faster ships—made sailing the coast of Africa to gather slaves easier. Improvements in medicine helped to keep more slaves alive on the horrible Atlantic crossing. Advances in agricultural science introduced new methods to grow more food for the increasing population.

In order to grow the huge amounts of sugarcane needed to satisfy Europe, large plantations covering hundreds of acres were developed. It was expensive to produce sugar, so the operation had to be large for the owner to get the best return on his investment. Sugarcane required lots of land and water, and processing plants had to be built close to the fields. Growers needed to know the best methods for growing this crop since extracting the sugar from the cane was complicated. In addition, the slaves and indentured servants needed somewhere to live, so buildings and food had to be provided. The changing market demands were also a constant concern to the sugar planters.

The Atlantic slave trade lasted for nearly 400 years. Ships would leave Europe filled with materials—textiles, weapons, pots and pans, and tools—that could be traded for slaves. On the west coast of Africa, slaves, mainly young men in their prime, were loaded onto the ships. They were unloaded in the Caribbean, where the ships were filled with sugar, hides, tobacco, and cotton for the return trip to Europe. This triangular movement was simple and quick, and made many European families rich.

It is estimated that as many as 1.5 million slaves were transported by the French[3] and 540,000 by the Dutch to their colonies in the Caribbean[4], but Great Britain had the largest slave society. At its height, at the end of the 1700s, slaves made up about 80 percent of the population of the British territories in the Caribbean, at nearly 3.5 million.[5]

The brutality of slavery gave rise to many slave rebellions and revolts. The most successful slave revolts took place in Haiti during the revolution of 1791 through 1804. This was an uprising against both slavery and French colonial rule. When the revolution was over, Haiti was the first modern republic led by people of African descent.

The end of Caribbean slavery was due to several factors. The frequency of revolts meant colonial powers had to provide costly military assistance to plantation owners. Machines to help with sugar cultivation decreased the need for slaves. In Europe the feeling that slavery was morally wrong was growing. Finally, over the course of about 75 years, slavery was outlawed, then abolished on all the Caribbean islands altogether by 1879. The end of slavery, however, did not lead to the end of colonialism. Most of the islands remained colonies, not independent states, until the 1970s and 1980s.

Colonialism in the Caribbean went through different phases or stages. The period of exploration between Columbus's arrival and the 1700s was the first period. The period of slavery was a second stage. The end of slavery marked a transition to a new stage, in which the colonizers still maintained political control, commanded economic resources, and held stereotypical and often negative ideas of black people as having low intelligence, little morality, and considerable physical strength.

Along with the end of slavery and independence in the Caribbean came several problems. Europeans and native inhabitants alike had to face the weakness of Caribbean economies, which had been developed upon the basis of single-crop exports to the world market. The resources of the colonizers were increasingly limited, as they lost their status as world powers. In addition, there were changing ideas about how societies should be governed. Over time, the colonial countries, which once had absolute power, began to grant some limited powers of self-government to the people of their colonies. Political arrangements varied from colony to colony. For example, Barbados and the Bahamas had independent legislatures, overseen by British governors, while Jamaica and most of the other British colonies were governed more directly by Great Britain as Crown colonies.

During the 1800s, the United States had made clear its interest in the Caribbean, first through the Monroe Doctrine of 1823, which stated that European powers were no longer

After the government of the Dominican Republic accumulated massive foreign debt, U.S. president Theodore Roosevelt announced the Roosevelt Corollary, an amendment to the Monroe Doctrine. This extension asserted the right of the United States to intervene in the economic affairs of the Caribbean and Central America if they were unable to pay their international debts. It was deemed necessary to keep European nations out of Latin America. Later, presidents used the corollary as justification for U.S. intervention in Cuba, Nicaragua, Haiti, and the Dominican Republic.

allowed to colonize within the Americas or interfere with the affairs of the newly independent states of the Americas. The United States also agreed not to interfere with existing colonies or their dependencies in the Western Hemisphere. The United States exercised both "gunboat" (military) and "dollar" (economic) diplomacy to strengthen its control of the region. The United States especially wielded its power in Cuba, Haiti, and the Dominican Republic, developing some aspects of those societies but also creating considerable nationalist opposition to U.S. presence and power.

AFTER WORLD WAR II

World War II increased the influence of the United States and decreased the role of the colonial powers, which were occupied in a war on their own continent. As the war progressed, the United States seized land in Cuba, Haiti, and the Dominican Republic for military bases. Great Britain allowed the United States to use some of its Caribbean bases in exchange for war materials, further cementing American involvement in the region. After World War II, as the Cold War rivalry between the U.S.-led bloc of market democracies and the Soviet-led bloc of Communist states unfolded, the United States continued to have a strong strategic, as well as economic interest, in the region. The Caribbean was a site of major cargo sea lanes (routes used by ships important for trading by sea) and a source of important raw minerals. Cuba was positioned directly in the Caribbean Basin, as were other countries in which there were rivalries between parties and movements closer to the U.S.-led bloc and others identified more as neutral, socialist, or Communist-aligned.

During and after World War II, nationalist sentiment—the idea that people in the colonies should be self-governing—grew. The decline in income and growth of poverty united Caribbean leaders, who created independent labor unions and worked for improvements in working conditions and wages, education, health care, and safe water. While investigating protests in the 1930s a high-level British group, the West India Royal Commission, recommended that not only white landowners but all adults should have the right to vote.[6]

Men from the British Caribbean fought alongside the British in World War II against fascism and racism. The 1941 Atlantic Charter, which established a vision for a post-World War II world, was drafted by British prime minister Winston

(continues on page 18)

THE CARIBBEAN DIASPORA

The history of the Caribbean is framed by two diasporas. A diaspora is a mass migration, or a scattering of peoples away from their homelands. Diasporas usually occur when people's homes are conquered or colonized, when people are captured and traded as slaves, when people are persecuted and must flee, or when economic prospects at home are poor and other places offer better work opportunities.

The global sugar trade, which brought slaves and indentured laborers to Caribbean shores, created the first important diaspora that shaped the Caribbean. This diaspora involved a scattering of the peoples of Africa and later Asia to the Caribbean (and elsewhere). Caribbean poet, Derek Walcott, describes this dislocation when he writes, "Something inside is laid wide like a wound, / some open passage that has cleft the brain, / some deep, amnesiac blow. We left / somewhere a life that we never found / customs and gods that are not born again".*

In the more recent period, and especially since World War II, there has been a scattering away of the Caribbean peoples from their homelands. For example, many people who lived in British colonies migrated to the United Kingdom, because they were in need of more workers after the war. When they were no longer needed, in the early 1960s, the United Kingdom began to oppose immigration, and numbers began to shift to the United States and Canada. Today, large numbers of people from the Caribbean islands of Cuba, the Dominican Republic, Haiti, Jamaica, and Guyana go to the United States, the United Kingdom, Canada, the Netherlands, and France looking for better opportunities.

Many of the home countries are developing nations. Immigrant workers have made a big contribution to their home economies, because they tend to send most of their money back to their families. This money totals more than what their countries' businesses invest back into these nations and also more than what they get in economic development assistance from wealthier countries. This money helps many poor family members who would have difficulty making ends meet without it.

There has also been negative impact on the Caribbean nations. It is often the highly skilled and well educated who leave the region, depleting the Caribbean of critical human resources. The most talented are in demand and can afford to migrate. Among those leaving, women often outnumber men, and many children are left behind with relatives or family friends until migrating parents are sure of their place in the new society or return to their homeland.

Caribbean immigration has also had a positive effect on the new countries. Caribbean entrepreneurs, scientists, and teachers help create good economic and social links between countries. Caribbean peoples bring with them their traditions, language, food, and culture and introduce them to their new societies. For example, many big cities in North America and Europe have a Caribbean carnival that is modeled on the one found in Trinidad and Tobago. Carnival in Trinidad and Tobago has its roots in West African festivals, where slaves added music, dancing, and singing to a conservative celebration of the end of crop season. Today, people from all over the world flock here to see the elaborate costumes, music competitions, and parades. The Notting Hill carnival in London attracts about 2 million people over three days each year.

---

* Quoted in Ruel Johnson, "The Diaspora," Caribbean Community. Available online at *http://www.caricom.org/jsp/projects/uwicaricomproject/caribbean_ diaspora.jsp.*

(continued from page 15)

Churchill and U.S. president Franklin D. Roosevelt. It called for self-determination and free trade for all peoples and turned out to be the first step toward the creation of the United Nations. This agreement gave hope to leaders in the British colonies and elsewhere that they might see progress in terms of national autonomy.

European leaders began to lose interest in their Caribbean colonies because they saw the region as one that would always be poor with little room for expanding industry and thought that the economic benefits no longer outweighed the costs. In Great Britain, the physical destruction and economic collapse resulting from World War II made rebuilding at home and release from colonial obligations high priorities.

After World War II, the European colonial powers made an effort to improve the economies of the region. The war had already disrupted overseas trade, forcing the colonies to become more economically self-reliant by growing more of their own food and producing more goods. Some industries, such as limestone quarrying, provided materials that were used both locally and overseas. The British Colonial Office granted land to small farmers and set up agencies to give advice about crops. The colonial office also granted plantation owners subsidies for repairs to machinery and for improved irrigation.

The idea of turning the area into a tourist retreat also began to take hold. As the island economies moved steadily away from reliance on export trade, tourism was seen as a way to create income that would further the economic development of the islands. Tourism would help alleviate the high unemployment rate while taking advantage of the islands' natural beauty and warm climate. The region's economy improved with America's presence, as local workers found employment and on-the-job training on military bases and at other facilities. Unemployment rates dropped and wages rose.

The British did not intend to create a crowd of small independent island states in the Caribbean. In their eyes, the creation of a federation of the smaller colonial units would be a better way to achieve decolonization and would also be more practical. Power would be divided between a central Caribbean government and the smaller units. In 1958, the West Indian Federation, which included the larger islands and some of the smaller ones, was established, still under the partial control of the British. It was this experiment that provided the first experience of political cooperation among the different small colonial entities. However, the West Indies Federation did not last long. Finally, in the 1960s and 1970s, many Caribbean nations achieved their independence as separate countries, though a few remained British dependencies.

In 1946, Guadeloupe and Martinique became overseas departments of France, sending representatives to the French National Assembly and Senate, France's main law-making bodies. Today, they are also members of the European Union and use the euro as their currency. Cuba and Puerto Rico are also part of the geographic Caribbean Basin. Cuba, in the northern Caribbean, won formal independence from Spain in 1902, fell under U.S. influence, then endured a tumultuous history ending in the 1959 revolution led by Fidel Castro. Puerto Rico was a long-time Spanish and then U.S. colony, which became a self-governing territory of the United States in 1952.

AFTER POLITICAL INDEPENDENCE

The independent states in the Caribbean and in CARICOM remain small. Many fit into an official category of "small state" recognized by the World Bank and other international agencies. Small states have populations under 1.5 million, as well as limited territorial size and limited gross domestic product (the dollar value of goods and services produced within a country in a year). According to a report by the World Bank, the Caribbean is the world's largest group of small states,[7] with 12 countries categorized as such: Antigua and Barbuda, the Bahamas, Barbados, Belize, Dominica, Grenada, Guyana, St. Kitts and Nevis, St. Lucia, St. Vincent and the Grenadines,

While the rise of tourism has sparked indirect growth in other industries, such as construction and other service- and tourism-related activities, many islands are beginning to diversify their industries. Several islands supplement their tourism dollars by exporting products like coffee (Dominican Republic), bauxite (Jamaica), and nutmeg (Grenada). Above, these plant workers peel red-colored mace from husked nutmeg seeds in Charlotte Town, Grenada.

Suriname, and Trinidad and Tobago. Despite their similarities in size and culture, they differ in terms of their degree of economic development. For instance, the Bahamas, Antigua and Barbuda, and Barbados, with a per capita income of $14,000, are considered high-income countries. The more than 770,000 residents of Guyana earn, on average, less than $4,000 per year. As such, Guyana is considered a low-income country.[8]

Economically, these states tend to depend upon imports and the tourist trade. They often have trouble adapting to changing global economic conditions because of their size, limited economic resources, and sometimes remote locations.

The populations of such states also have health problems, including a rise in HIV/AIDS cases, and challenges related to education, unemployment, and youth. Various world organizations such as the World Bank, the United Nations, the World Trade Organization, the International Monetary Fund, and the European Union work closely with these small states to help find solutions to the problems they face.

The small states of the Caribbean experienced a long period of colonialism in which their economies were selectively developed and their societies were controlled and restructured in the interests of the colonial powers. Therefore, it is not surprising that they are still developing countries, or countries that rely heavily upon agriculture or mineral extraction, and do not have a strong industrial base or a strong position in the world economy. General living standards are lower than in the wealthy industrialized countries, and resources available to governments to provide education and health services to the population are limited.

The Caribbean is also a product of a complex history of transplanted populations from all corners of the world. European settlers made the Caribbean a center of the slave trade, then introduced indentured servitude from many parts of Asia alongside the remaining native peoples of the region. In many Caribbean countries, racial and ethnic differences enrich the culture, while in a few they fragment societies and politics. Migration continues to characterize the region—migration among neighboring Caribbean countries and between the Caribbean and former colonial powers. Outward migration is often driven by poverty or violence and the hope for better opportunities elsewhere.

All of these aspects of Caribbean states pose challenges to the political leaders trying to manage and guide this area of the world, both in their individual states and through CARICOM.

History of CARICOM

Over time, the Caribbean's small countries realized that to overcome their shared history of domination by bigger countries, they would have to unite and find a way to share their future as free and independent states. Their ultimate goal was to individually and collectively establish better lives for their people—socially, economically, and politically. Although they decided to cooperate for the common good, agreeing on methods and approaches to cooperation would be challenging.

THE BRITISH EMPIRE AND THE BRITISH WEST INDIES FEDERATION

By the early 1900s, Great Britain controlled vast areas of the world, ruling about one-quarter of the world's population. Residents of the Caribbean Islands were no longer satisfied

On April 22, 1958, in Port of Spain in Trinidad and Tobago, the West Indies Federation was formally recognized as the newest member of the British Commonwealth. The ceremony inaugurating the federal legislature was officiated by Princess Margaret of Great Britain *(center)*. The federation, which comprised 24 main islands and more than 200 islets, cays, and minor islands, hoped to unite under one single government.

with outside rulers; they wanted to rule themselves. Local leaders believed that a union of the islands, at first under the British, was the first necessary step toward becoming independent. The British government also was moving toward granting independence to their colonies and thought that a larger political entity would be better than many small autonomous states.

In 1958, the British colonies of Antigua and Barbuda, Barbados, Dominica, Grenada, Jamaica, Montserrat, St. Kitts and Nevis, Anguilla, Saint Lucia, St. Vincent, and Trinidad and Tobago formed a political union called the British West Indies Federation. The capital of the federation was Port of Spain, in Trinidad and Tobago.

England's queen, Elizabeth II, was the head of the federation and had authority over the colonies within it. She appointed a governor-general from England, Patrick Buchan-Hepburn, to oversee the federation. The governor-general could veto any laws the federation passed.

The federation's House of Representatives elected 45 members, while the Senate comprised 19 members appointed by the governor-general after consulting the individual colony governments. The number of seats in the House was related to population, with Jamaica holding 17, Trinidad and Tobago 10, Barbados 5, Monserrat 1, and the other islands 2 each. A prime minister and 10 other officials would make up the cabinet, or what was known as the Council of State. As in Great Britain and other parliamentary democracies, the prime minister would be selected by those elected to the legislature and be the recognized leader of the party that won the most seats in the election. The prime minister was the head of the cabinet and had the right to appoint and dismiss other cabinet members.

To compete in the first election to the West Indies House of Representatives, two large, federation-wide political parties formed out of smaller parties that already existed in individual colonies. One, the West Indies Federal Labor Party (WIFLP), was comprised mainly of existing political parties based in the cities. The Democratic Labor Party (DLP) was made up mainly of political parties from rural areas. Both groups wanted to maintain and strengthen ties with Great Britain, the United States, and Canada. Both thought it was essential to obtain outside financial and technical aid to develop their countries and thought tourism was one way to generate revenue. Both also wanted to enlarge the federation by bringing in British Guiana (present-day Guyana) and British Honduras.

The similarities between the groups ended there. The WIFLP wanted to encourage the development of agriculture, bring into the federation the Bahamas as well as British Guiana and Honduras, establish a central bank for all of the small countries, and create strong self-government in each of the territories. The WIFLP supported labor unions and greater cooperation and equality in what they called democratic socialism. Conversely, the DLP attacked socialism, wanted to keep taxes low, and emphasized the larger West Indian unit more than self-government within the individual member units.

The WIFLP, which was popular mainly on the smaller islands, won the first election on March 25, 1958. It gained 26 seats, while its DLP rival won 19, mainly in Jamaica and Trinidad and Tobago. Sir Grantley Adams, leader of the WIFLP, became prime minister of the federation. He immediately had to deal with problems that included power struggles between the central, or federal, government and the individual governments of each island. The smaller islands were afraid of being overwhelmed by the larger islands—which had more money, land mass, people, and clout—while the larger provinces were worried about mass migrations from the smaller islands. In response, the federation denied freedom of movement between the islands. The federal government also had to function with a very small budget. In fact, the individual budgets of Jamaica and Trinidad and Tobago were larger than that of the government of the entire federation. This meant the central government had to rely on grants from Great Britain and contributions from individual member states. Jamaica and Trinidad and Tobago, being the largest members of the federation, contributed 85 percent of the budget to the federation and resented additional requests for funds.

Many other challenges faced the 10 colonies of the federation. Adams also had to contend with political egos. The individual leaders of the island nations were nationalists and well respected at home, so they were hesitant to compromise and think in terms of the region as a whole. The individual governments were unwilling to give up their autonomy to a central government.

Finally, Great Britain imposed strict rules for its administration, effectively continuing its colonial rule. The members had arguments about basic planning and taxation. These conflicts ultimately made it impossible to maintain any kind of a cooperative atmosphere in which the federation could succeed.

Still, within four years of the federation's existence, regional cooperation grew significantly and the central government saw many positive changes. The federation created a civil service, a group of governmental agencies that were able to work together. The federation also developed a relationship with Canada, which shared a similar colonial history with Great Britain. In friendship, the Canadian government gave the federation two merchant ships for transporting goods and passengers—the *Federal Palm* and the *Federal Maple*. These two ships formed the West Indies Regional Shipping Service and traveled between the member islands twice a month, creating an important link between the individual states.

Also under the federation's leadership, the University College of the West Indies added a campus in Jamaica, in addition to the one already established in Trinidad and another in Barbados. The university was established as a part of the University of London to serve the individual island nations of the Caribbean. Its official mission is to help "to propel the economic, social, political and cultural development of West Indian society through teaching, research, innovation, advisory and community services and intellectual leadership"[9] in the West Indies, allowing for more regional self-government.

Although it lasted only a short period, the federation was valuable practice for the island governments to learn to work together. They discovered strength in numbers and realized the need to continue the programs and practices that had resulted in unprecedented cooperation between the islands and the mainland.

The West Indies Federation dissolved in 1962. Many reasons were put forth, such as the lack of popular support, competing island nationalisms, the weakness of the federal government, feuding between political leaders, and the lack of history and experience with a common administration, among others. Still, most people point to Jamaica's dissatisfaction with the federation as the main reason for its demise. In a national referendum—or direct vote of the people—in Jamaica in 1961, the majority favored withdrawal. There seemed to be several reasons for people's antagonism. The people of Jamaica, the largest federation member and located hundreds of miles from the others, may have felt more self-sufficient and independent from the group. Also, Jamaica's share of seats in the federal parliament was smaller than its share of the total population of the federation, so many Jamaicans believed that the smaller nations were getting more attention, not pulling their weight financially, and even draining Jamaican wealth. The biggest reason for the island's dissatisfaction was the fact that the federation had not brought the colonies, and Jamaica in particular, closer to independence from Great Britain; Jamaican leaders felt that, on the contrary, the federation was holding back the movement toward independence.

On January 14, 1962, the People's National Movement (the Trinidad part of the WIFLP) passed a resolution rejecting any further involvement with the federation. Shortly thereafter, Jamaica gained full independence from Great Britain, on August 6, 1962, followed by Trinidad and Tobago on August 31. The remaining eight nations were simply unable to keep any semblance of a federation together after these countries withdrew, mainly for financial reasons. Again, they became colonies of Great Britain, and each earned its independence within the next 20 years.

AFTER THE FEDERATION: CARIFTA

In July 1963, Dr. Eric Williams, the first prime minister of Trinidad and Tobago, called a meeting of the Caribbean heads of governments to discuss the possibility of a different partnership. Dr. Williams told them:

> Small countries like ours encounter great difficulty in establishing their influence in the world dominated by power and regional associations. This general difficulty is aggravated in our case by centuries of subordination to outside control, which has given rise to a view not uncommon outside of the West Indies, that we are satellites by nature and exist only to serve as pawns to outside countries. We have therefore no alternative but to seek, against the background of our common history and traditions, to make common cause against the unfortunate tendency to regard us for all time as hewers of wood and drawers of water for other people.[10]

At a conference in July 1965, leaders agreed to establish a free trade area in the Caribbean and called the organization to oversee it the Caribbean Free Trade Association (CARIFTA). An official agreement was signed on December 15, 1965. Countries belonging to this area would lower or remove taxes on imports coming from other countries within the region. They felt that as many Caribbean countries as possible should be included and that the free trade area would ultimately become known as the Caribbean Common Market, with the goal of developing regional economic cooperation.

CARIFTA was mainly a free trade organization, a group of countries that agreed to eliminate tariffs (taxes on imported items) and quotas (limits on the amount of items imported) on goods exchanged among themselves. Freer trade, economists thought, would increase trade among the member countries and expand the variety of goods and services that were traded.

Dr. Eric Williams was one of the most significant leaders in the modern history of Trinidad and Tobago. He formed and led one of the most important political parties in the country, the People's National Movement. Trinidad and Tobago joined the West Indies Federation, and Williams became the country's first prime minister (1956–1981). The country later withdrew from the organization and gained its independence from Great Britain in 1962.

Economic cooperation would also ensure fair competition, setting up similar rules for all members.

Member countries in CARIFTA could work together to develop the industries that the colonial powers had not, make agriculture more efficient, and tackle social problems like unemployment and poverty. If the Caribbean countries could speak with one voice in international trade, they might be able to achieve better terms for their exports. CARIFTA also planned to set standard tariffs for goods coming from outside the region. For example, cars from the United States imported to Jamaica would be taxed at the same level as cars imported to Barbados. This made CARIFTA not only a free trade area, but also a customs union. They felt that free trade should benefit its member states equally.

Twelve Commonwealth Caribbean countries ultimately joined CARIFTA: Antigua and Barbuda, Barbados, Belize,

ERIC WILLIAMS: THE FATHER OF THE NATION

Around 1900 Trinidad was a Crown colony of England, dependent on agriculture, and socially dominated by white French Creoles. Creole is a word used to refer to people of Amerindian, African, and European descent. Creoles are black, white, and brown peoples who created new societies that blended European forms of society with local cultures.

Thomas Henry Williams, a black postal worker, was a staunch Catholic with only a primary school education. Elisa Boissiere Williams was a member of the French Creole elite. Her father had been disinherited, leaving her with little money. On September 25, 1911, Eric Eustace was born. With 11 children in the family, life was hard, and many hopes rested on Eric.

Eric was a bright student who formed close relationships with some of his teachers, one of whom nurtured his love for history. He later attended England's Oxford University on scholarship, writing his Ph.D. thesis on the abolition of the West Indian slave trade and slavery and earned his degree in 1938. He took a job in Washington, D.C., at Howard University, where he established a relationship with another famous West Indian thinker and writer, C. L. R. James. In 1944, he wrote a controversial book *Capitalism and Slavery*, which

Dominica, Grenada, Guyana, Jamaica, Montserrat, St. Kitts and Nevis, Anguilla (Anguilla is now a separate British dependency), Saint Lucia, Trinidad and Tobago, and St. Vincent and the Grenadines. The group's goals were to promote and encourage the development of diverse trade, ensure fair competition between members, and encourage economic development.

In 1968, a secretariat was established to oversee CARIFTA. The secretariat was a department that carried out the administrative work for the organization including scheduling

argued that the British abolition of the Atlantic slave trade was not really due to an increase in humanitarian feelings among the English but instead due to economic reasons. Many researchers have questioned this perspective; however, it remains an important one today.

In 1948, Williams returned to Trinidad as deputy chairman of the Caribbean Research Council, and in 1956 he founded a new political party, the People's National Movement (PNM). The PNM was highly organized and won many seats in the legislative council, allowing Williams to become what was then called the chief minister. The PNM partnered with the Federal Labor Party (FLP) in the 1958 West Indies Federation elections, but the FLP lost. Some say this may have led to Williams's disenchantment with the organization. After Jamaica left the West Indies Federation, he encouraged Trinidad and Tobago's withdrawal from the organization in 1962, leading to the dissolution of the federation. Ultimately, this led to Trinidad's winning its independence in August 1962. He was elected prime minister and served from 1961–1981. Williams is credited with launching several ambitious plans to develop Trinidad's economy, attracting foreign investment through tax incentives, and securing aid from wealthier countries.

meetings and setting the agendas. In October 1969, in an effort to assist member countries in financing their social and economic programs, the Caribbean Development Bank was established. Headquartered in Bridgetown, Barbados, its goal is to promote private and public investment and encourage economic and business development and support regional and local banks.

FROM CARIFTA TO CARICOM

In April 1973, at the eighth annual heads of government meeting, the Caribbean leaders signed the Georgetown Accord, which announced that a new Caribbean Community and Common Market (CARICOM, now called just the Caribbean Community) would replace CARIFTA. The official enforce-

MEMBERS OF CARICOM AND DATE JOINED

FULL MEMBERS

Antigua and Barbuda *(July 4, 1974)*
Bahamas *(July 4, 1983)*
Barbados *(August 1, 1973)*
Belize *(May 1, 1974)*
Dominica *(May 1, 1974)*
Grenada *(May 1, 1974)*
Guyana *(August 1, 1973)*
Haiti *(provisional membership July 4, 1998; full membership July 2, 2002)*
Jamaica *(August 1, 1973)*
Montserrat *(May 1, 1974)*
Saint Kitts and Nevis *(July 26, 1974)*
Saint Lucia *(May 1, 1974)*
Saint Vincent and the Grenadines *(May 1, 1974)*
Suriname *(July 4, 1995)*
Trinidad and Tobago *(August 1, 1973)*

ASSOCIATES

Anguilla *(July 1999)*
Bermuda *(July 2, 2003)*
British Virgin Islands *(July 1991)*
Cayman Islands *(May 16, 2002)*
Turks and Caicos Islands *(July 1991)*

OBSERVERS

Aruba
Colombia
Dominican Republic
Mexico
Netherlands Antilles
Puerto Rico
Venezuela

ment of CARICOM took place on July 4, 1973, with the signing of the Treaty of Chaguaramas in Trinidad. The first four Caribbean islands to gain their independence—Barbados, Guyana, Jamaica, and Trinidad and Tobago—signed the treaty. Currently, CARICOM has 15 full members, 5 associate members (who participate in "functional cooperation" areas of the community including education, health, and sports, but do not have voting rights), and 7 observers.

The Caribbean nations hoped to strengthen regional cooperation beyond CARIFTA. They wanted to strengthen or deepen the areas in which they had started work and expand into new areas. The main objectives were to strengthen the common market and integrate further the small island economies into a larger regional one. A second objective was functional cooperation, or the pooling of resources and sharing of services in areas of human and social development, such as education, health, and environmental protection. Finally, they wanted to coordinate their policies in world politics, presenting a united front in dealings with countries outside the grouping.

In 1989, the heads of government announced the Grand Anse Declaration, which expressed their determination to work toward a single market and economy—one economic space comprised of the national economies and markets of all the member states. This general objective is referred to as the CARICOM Single Market and Economy (CSME). It includes free movement of goods and services, the right of businesses to set up in any member state, a common external tariff, free movement of money and wealth, and the free movement of workers. CARICOM nations signed a revised treaty in 2001 taking these objectives into account.

The overall goals of CARICOM include economic development or prosperity, social improvements, and national protection and security. The specific meaning of these goals has changed in the decades since the formation of the organization in 1973, and member states have had to adjust their priorities.

At the Conference on the Caribbean, held in Washington, D.C. in 2007, CARICOM, the academic community, business leaders, and policymakers addressed the need to take specific steps to achieve the long-term goals of improving the lives of the Caribbean people. President George Bush (*center*, pictured with Caribbean leaders) acknowledged the significant contributions the Caribbean people have made to the United States.

Some countries have faced long economic crises, while others have had changing economic prospects due to fluctuating demand for natural resources and products. New issues have appeared on the agenda with the changing needs of the member states: cooperation in resolving disputed territory, the possibility of a Caribbean currency (similar to the euro in Europe), major initiatives in environmental cooperation, and major initiatives to control the illegal drug trade. Some countries, like Haiti, continue to experience political upheaval. Still another challenge is the ability to keep up with technological advances in telecommunications and electronic communications.

On July 4, 2008, CARICOM celebrated its thirty-fifth anniversary. The president of Guyana, Bharrat Jagdeo, spoke about what being a member of CARICOM means to his people and how the ideals and principles of the original treaty remain relevant in a constantly changing world:

> The enormous challenges associated with the rapid shift in the global economy, climate change, and the rising energy and food prices will not affect the vision of our founding fathers for a united Caribbean Community... I wish to urge that we continue to summon up our collective strengths and draw on our diversity to craft a closer regional integration and a Community which will reflect the political, economic and cultural realities of our region.[11]

Because of the islands' colonial history, the Caribbean's political leaders remain cautious in their approaches to integration and cooperation. They want to ensure that their countries retain their individuality while the governments attempt to build a single unit to address their common goals. At the same time, even though the countries vary in size, population, and income levels, their colonial history brings a commonality that binds them in a brotherhood. The West Indies Federation, which led to CARIFTA and finally CARICOM, has played a major part in creating this bond, leading to a stronger foundation for the growth and stabilization of the countries' economies, social welfare structures, and trade.

How CARICOM Works

Since CARICOM is a voluntary organization among independent states, it has few ways to compel member countries to carry out its decisions. The goals of the organization are many and far-reaching, and each country has the opportunity to voice its opinions.

AT THE TOP

CARICOM has two main governing bodies—the Conference of the Heads of Government and the Community Council of Ministers. The Conference is comprised of the prime ministers from each member state and is regarded as the supreme decision-making body of the community, setting general policy direction. They make financial and policy decisions and finalize treaties between CARICOM and other countries. The chairmanship of the conference rotates among all the prime ministers. Each state has one vote in the conference, so that any one state can veto a decision.

On July 5, 2001, at the twenty-second meeting of the conference in the Bahamas, the heads of government signed a Revised Treaty of Chaguaramas, in order to establish a single market and economy (Caribbean Single Market Economy, or CSME) for the region. This issue is so important that they assigned lead responsibility to the prime minister of Barbados and created regional committees to be overseen by council ministers. The prime minister of Antigua and Barbuda is in charge of service issues; labor issues are overseen by the prime minister of Dominica; the prime minister of Jamaica heads trade negotiations with countries outside CARICOM; and the prime minister of Saint Lucia oversees governance and justice within CSME.

CARICOM also has a prime ministerial subcommittee on cricket—what might come closest to being the Caribbean national sport—played with a bat and ball and two teams of 11 players. This subcommittee was established in 1996 to determine how West Indies cricket and cricket players (cricketers) could be supported on an ongoing basis. As of 2004, the prime ministers of Antigua and Barbuda, Dominica, Grenada, and Jamaica were official members of this subcommittee, but all heads of government were invited to join if they were interested.

The second top body, the Community Council, oversees all strategic planning and is comprised of government officials from each member state who manage Caribbean community affairs for their nation. This council is responsible for approving programs and proposals developed by other community committees, examining and approving the community budget, ensuring the operation and development of the CSME. Here, too, decisions must be made unanimously.

Other Decision-making Bodies

The Conference of Heads of Government and the Community Council of Ministers are assisted by four more ministers councils, three bodies of the community, and a secretariat which carries out decisions. The Council for Trade and Economic Development is responsible for promoting trade and economic development of the community. It oversees progress toward the CSME. The Council for Foreign and Community Relations is responsible for relations with states outside of CARICOM and international organizations such as the United Nations agencies. The Council for Human and Social Development is charged with promoting improvements in health, education, labor and industrial relations, youth, women, and sports. The Council for Finance and Planning coordinates economic policy and takes steps toward unifying economic policies in the region.

The three other groups form a committee that gives legal advice to the community; a committee that overseas CARICOM's budget; and a committee of top bankers, the Central Bank Governors, that advise CARICOM on certain economic issues.

THE SECRETARIAT AND THE SECRETARY-GENERAL

The secretariat of CARICOM is an administrative body, not a decision-making one. It works to carry out the decisions made by higher bodies and generally oversees the operation of CARICOM. The staff is employed by CARICOM and includes planners and managers, technical experts, and office workers from all the member states. All of CARICOM's administrative work is handled within the secretariat, including oversight of community relations, regional trade, and social development programs. Those who work within the secretariat must ensure that decisions are followed and fully reported to all members.

They have to help member states meet their established goals for participation in CARICOM and must have all information pertaining to CARICOM's objectives ready to disseminate. They must help put into practice the approved CARICOM programs to meet the organization's broader goals, as well as draft the budgets that will help finance them and coordinate the different regional, national, and international agencies and organizations that will carry them out. The members of the secretariat hold very important positions as the eyes, ears, arms, and legs of the community at large. They must ensure that what is supposed to get done, does get done—on time, within the budget, and according to high standards.

The secretary-general, who heads the secretariat, manages a large staff. Even though the secretary-general is more a coordinator and manager than a major political decision-maker, he or she plays an important leadership role in holding the organization together and explaining it to external bodies and agencies. CARICOM has had six secretaries-general, beginning with Fred Cozier from Barbados, in 1968, while the organization was still CARIFTA.

Edwin Carrington of Trinidad and Tobago has served as secretary-general since 1992. When Carrington took office, the institutions of CARICOM were beginning to change. The objectives of CARICOM were expanding, and many were saying that CARICOM had ambitious plans but was unable to carry them through. "CARICOM needs to be nimble and flexible and cannot rely on structures which have remained virtually unchanged for over 20 years,"[12] said Carrington, encouraging organizational change to make the group more effective.

Carrington took over the leadership position just as the Soviet Union was breaking up and international politics was changing the way people thought about the Caribbean. At the same time, international trade and the global economy were getting more competitive. CARICOM's objectives continue to

Dr. Edwin Carrington faced many challenges and urgent tasks when he assumed the position of secretary-general of CARICOM in 1992. Carrington has been charged with overseeing major structural changes to ensure that CARICOM can compete in the global economy, lifting the profile of the community and its people, and responding to the AIDS epidemic and the rising problem of terrorism.

expand as, more recently, Carrington leads the organization during the Caribbean AIDS epidemic and in a world newly concerned with global terrorism.

Carrington brings to the secretariat a great deal of experience and knowledge. A former economist with a focus on West Indian economic development and Caribbean integration, he has managed to bring the organization together with Asian and Pacific countries while negotiating trade rules with Europe.

Other Regional Bodies

Other groups work toward advancement on environmental issues and regional integration. These include:

- The Meteorological Organization
- The Disaster Emergency Response Agency
- The Organization for Standards and Quality
- The Center for Developmental Administration
- The Institutes for Environmental Health, Agricultural Research, Food and Nutrition, Meteorology and Hydrology
- The Caribbean Development Bank
- Examination Council
- Law Institute
- The Organization of Eastern Caribbean States

THE CARIBBEAN COURT OF JUSTICE

The Caribbean Court of Justice (CCJ) was established in 2001 mainly to help with the development of the CSME. Its main job is to interpret and uphold the provisions included in the revised Treaty of Chaguaramas, which included a major commitment to the single market and economy. The creation of a single economy across many countries with pre-existing economies and laws is complicated, and the CSME creates many new rights and obligations for states that signed the treaty. These rights and obligations relate to setting up businesses, providing professional services, moving wealth from country to country, and buying land for businesses. Prior to the establishment of this new CCJ, there was a procedure written into CARICOM law for resolving these kinds of legal disputes. Unfortunately, it was never used, and serious disputes were never settled. This state of affairs slowed down the process of economic integration and diminished commitment to CARICOM. It made international investors in the Caribbean economy wary. The CCJ's supporters hope

Members of a 10-member panel posed for photographs during the installation ceremony of the Caribbean Court of Justice (CCJ) in 2003. This panel was installed to select judges for the CCJ. The CCJ was developed in response to a call for a permanent regional court, in order to strengthen the Caribbean legal system and to promote social and economic stability.

that this new international court will strengthen CARICOM and the CSME.[13]

A second, more controversial aspect of this court is that it is also designed to act as an appeals court for the local and national legal systems in individual countries, a supreme court of appeal. In this respect, it is described as a "municipal court of last resort." The court is designed to review and rule on appeals from civil and criminal cases originating in the courts of individual countries.

The appeals court in the British-speaking countries of the region prior to the creation of the CCJ had been the privy council of the United Kingdom, a court which is part of the British judicial system and the highest court for certain cases in Great Britain. (Guyana had its own court of appeal, and Dutch-speaking Suriname and French- and Creole-speaking Haiti were also outside the British court's jurisdiction.) There was quite a bit of general concern in the region that their legal systems still granted such power to a British institution whose power stemmed from the colonial era.

Two court cases increased Caribbean dissatisfaction with the privy council. In one, the privy council refused to allow capital punishment for persons convicted of murder, commuting the sentences of two Jamaican death row inmates to life, even though the majority in the local community supported the death penalty. In another, the privy council granted a license to operate a radio station to a company without the approval of the national government. But many in the Caribbean remain attached to the high standard of professionalism and the legal traditions of the British courts. Human rights organizations in the Caribbean worry that the CCJ will bring back "hanging." This part of the new court's jurisdiction has been controversial, with Barbados and Guyana among the first member states to agree to transfer the appeal function to the new court.[14]

The seven judges of the CCJ are appointed by the Regional Judicial and Legal Services Commission. The nine members of this commission are not members of any political party or governmental agency, but rather come from a variety of civil organizations. They are responsible for choosing judges and also responsible for dismissing them. As part of their participation in the CCJ, the member states must sign an agreement that they will enforce the court's rulings in their own country.

CARICOM
Economies

CARICOM ECONOMIES ARE SMALL AND DEPEND UPON IMPORTS and exports. The standard of living, as measured in GDP, or gross domestic product per capita (the total size of the economy divided by population), is limited but varies from country to country. The majority of the population is poorer than those living in economically wealthy democracies in North America and Europe, but better off on the whole than the populations of sub-Saharan Africa and South Asia. CARICOM countries, like most small economies, struggle to meet the economic, educational, and health needs of their populations and with making their way in a competitive global economy.

TOURISM

Tourism in the Caribbean significantly impacts the region's economies, cultures, and ecosystems. The tourist industry has become so important to this region that it has replaced agriculture as the primary economic sector in the Caribbean. In 2000, tourism accounted for almost half of the GDP of Caribbean nations, while agriculture had shrunk to contributing about 8 percent. For example, the tourism industry accounts for about 70 percent of the economy of Nassau and Paradise Island in the Bahamas, with more than 50,000 people working in the sector.[15] About 70 percent of all workers are employed in the service sector in the Cayman Islands, while only 2 percent were in agriculture.[16] Tourism is also the biggest industry in Barbados. Residents find good jobs in the many hotels, restaurants, and shops that cater to the tourist trade.

People from all over the world flock to the Caribbean for many reasons. The Caribbean Islands offer diverse landscapes, good food, and many things to do. St. Kitts and Nevis is a destination for many cruise ships because of its natural deep-water harbor. Ships from various cruise lines steam into the ports of Basseterre and Charlestown, and passengers take tours to view Mount Liamuiga, a dormant volcano, or travel in the dense forest of Nevis where green vervet monkeys chatter in the tree-tops. Additional positive aspects of the Caribbean include the fact that the region is fairly free of insects, and North American and European visitors often share a common language with the Caribbean people: French, English, Dutch, and Spanish.

Ecological tourism, also known as ecotourism, is becoming increasingly popular with vacationers traveling to the Caribbean. Ecotourism focuses on social responsibility, volunteering, and learning new ways to live on the planet. This type of travel involves taking a trip to destinations where plant and

THE REGION'S ECONOMICS

COUNTRY	POPULATION (MILLIONS)	TOTAL GDP (IN BILLION U.S. DOLLARS EQUIVALENTS)	GDP/CAPITA (IN U.S. DOLLAR EQUIVALENT, ADJUSTED FOR PURCHASING POWER)	POVERTY (PERCENT OF POPULATION THAT IS EXTREMELY POOR)	HUMAN DEVELOPMENT (HEALTH, EDUCATION INCOME) RANK (1 IS BEST IN THE WORLD, 177 IS WORST)
Antigua and Barbuda	0.1 (2005)	0.9 (2005)	$1,250 (2005)	—	57 (2007)
The Bahamas	0.3 (2005)	5.5 (2005)	$ 18,380 (2005)	—	49 (2007)
Barbados	0.3 (2005)	3.1 (2005)	$ 17,297 (2005)	3	31 (2007)
Belize	0.3 (2005)	1.1 (2005)	$ 7,109 (2005)	17.5	80 (2007)
Dominica	0.1 (2005)	0.3 (2005)	$ 6,393 (2005)		71 (2007)
Grenada	0.1 (2005)	0.5 (2005)	$ 7, 843 (2005)		82 (2007)
Guyana	0.7 (2005)	0.8 (2005)	$ 4, 508 (2005)	14	97 (2007)
Haiti	9.3 (2005)	4.3 (2005)	$ 1,663 (2005)	35.4	146 (2007)
Jamaica	2.7 (2005)	9.6 (2005)	$ 4,291 (2005)	14.3	101 (2007)
Montserrat					
St. Kitts and Nevis	—	0.5 (2005)	$ 13,307 (2005)	—	54 (2007)
St. Lucia	0.2 (2005)	0.8 (2005)	$ 6,707 (2005)	6.5	72 (2007)
St.Vincent and Grena-dines	0.1 (2005)	0.4 (2005)	$ 6,568 (2005)	—	92 (2007)
Suriname	0.5 (2005)	1.3 (2005)	$ 7,722 (2005)	10.2	85 (2007)
Trinidad and Tobago	1.3 (2005)	14.4 (2005)	$ 14,603 (2005)	7.3	59 (2007)

Source: UNDP tables (www.undp.org)

Millions of tourists vacation in the Caribbean annually. The Caribbean offers the common languages that Europeans and North Americans speak (English, French, Dutch, or Spanish), lots of outdoor activities, and beautiful surroundings. The Caribbean Islands now depend on tourism for their economy. Above, vendors at the craft market in Nassau, Bahamas, sell their colorful straw goods.

animal life and cultural heritage are the primary attractions. Ecotourism has added another dimension to the tourist trade in the past 10 or 20 years. Private tour companies set visitors up with trips deep into the forest for treetop zip-line tours, bird-watching forays, or trips to experience the sights and scents of dozens of tropical flowers. National parks, where the land is protected, provide educational programs and a wide variety of things to see and do. Visitors explore the rainforests of Guyana or scuba dive among the many reefs of Dominica and Belize while preserving the natural environment.

There are also many dangers to relying so heavily on tourism. Tourism contributes less to the Caribbean economy in the long-term. Visitors from more developed countries expect to have the same amenities that they do back home, bringing an additional expense to the Caribbean. It is costly to maintain the infrastructure and the Caribbean governments have had to borrow money from foreign governments. These loans have stretched the limits of these less developed nations and their taxpayers, and some have required bailouts from the International Monetary Fund.[17]

Tourism has also brought higher prices for food, land, and other goods. Land for hotels and other tourist facilities is sold at an inflated price, making its cost out of reach for locals. In fact, most natives cannot afford to live along the beautiful coastline because the land has been bought by hotels and resorts. One island, Barbados, has decided to take action. Windows to the Sea, a local group, sought to establish a number of openings to the sea from the public highway, not only to create views of the ocean, but also to establish coastal and beach facilities and raise public awareness of the land use policies of the island.[18]

The tourism industry has also had a negative impact on Caribbean culture. In its effort to attract visitors to the island, people have complained that Trinidad's carnival has become inauthentic and commercialized. Even the indigenous culture of Costa Rica has now been adjusted to include Western food, music, and style.

AGRICULTURE

Sugar was the Caribbean's main export for decades, but the industry suffered after slavery was abolished. It still is the primary export of some countries, including Belize. In the 1950s, about 2,000 acres of northern Belize was planted with sugarcane, and today about 40,000 acres grow sugar, which accounts for about 60 percent of that country's agricultural exports. Belize's other agricultural exports include citrus, bananas, and seafood.

Individual countries focus on a few crops that provide them a strong return—nutmeg and mace in Grenada; rice in Guyana; coffee in Haiti; plantains and sweet potatoes in St. Vincent and the Grenadines; and flowers and flowering plants in Saint Lucia. Manufacturing based on agricultural products is also important in some member states. Milling of rice and flour and beer brewing are important in St. Vincent and the Grenadines; Guyana grows and exports both raw sugar and rice and processed and refined versions; and Dominica manufactures soap from the coconuts it grows in abundance. Jamaica relies on sugar processing, together with tourism, manufacturing, and bauxite mining.

Ironically, however, this historically agricultural region is facing an agricultural crisis and food shortages. Across the region, countries that formerly exported food now must import it at a cost of nearly $3 billion annually, partly because agriculture was neglected for tourism but also because food exports were emphasized at the expense of agriculture to feed local populations. While world food prices were low, the decline of Caribbean agriculture did not pose such a serious problem for the population. But now that food prices around the world are rising, that is no longer the case. Jamaica, for example, which once produced a half million pounds of rice annually, now must import much of this staple to meet the needs of its residents as well as the 2 million tourists who visit the island each year.[19] In Haiti hunger constantly stalks many children and adults, and the rising prices of rice and other products have provoked desperate street protests. The rise in world food prices threatens to reverse the progress that some Caribbean countries have made in decreasing extreme poverty.

Poor people are disproportionately affected by rising food prices because they spend a larger part of their income on food. Some factors that have caused an increase in prices include reduced production due to climate change, historically low level of food stocks, and increased demand for biofuels production. Haiti especially has become dependent on imported food for its survival. Above, this girl receives food from a UN peacekeeper in Port-au-Prince, Haiti.

FISHING

Since the CARICOM countries are surrounded by seas, fish and marine products are another important economic sector. Fishing always has been a large part of island life in the Caribbean, and certain plantation slaves were even specially groomed for fishing. Today, fishermen harvest up to a half million tons of fish a year of up to 170 different species for local consumption and export. Fishing, including sport fishing, is profitable for the islands, contributing millions of dollars to the islands' economies.[20]

Many varieties of fish feed tourists and island residents alike—snapper, king fish, flying fish, mahi mahi, shrimp, conch, and lobster. In fact, the lobsters fished in the Caribbean are valued at about $40 million a year.[21] Even so, since 2000, the number of fish caught in the region has dropped, and sellers have had to raise their prices. The sea is being over-fished, and environmental factors, including climate change, have impacted the supply. Conch, for example, has been listed as endangered by the Convention on International Trade in Endangered Species. Coral reefs, seagrass beds, and mangrove swamps shelter some fish, but as more coastal land is cleared for development these habitats are being damaged. As temperatures rise globally and sea levels rise, the decreasing amount of light reaching the coral reefs and seagrass beds will result in the death of that coral and then the death of certain fish species that rely on these reefs and beds for food sources.[22]

Fish farms, an alternative to open sea fishing, are increasing. In Guyana, fish farming (as opposed to catching fish in naturally occurring open waters) is important to the economy. The fish raised in farms not only help feed Guyanans but are also exported to the United States and Europe. The government of Guyana contributed to developing this industry by culturing fish along the coast, in flooded farm fields and sugar plantations, and on other unused land. Another CARICOM state working actively to increase fish production is Trinidad and Tobago, where the fishing industry accounts for more than half of the country's economy. Building fisheries and cultivating fish creates a new problem—water and land pollution of the fields and ponds used for this industry. Reducing pollution and harvesting only the amount of fish that will not deplete the fish population will help the Caribbean's fisheries.

BANKING AND FINANCE

International business and offshore banking are two financial sectors that have taken hold on some of the islands and continue to grow. Bermuda, an associate member of CARICOM since 2003, has an economy based almost entirely on international business and tourism, with finance constituting the largest sector.[23] Financial services also play a major role in the economy of the Cayman Islands. With $1.5 trillion in banking liabilities and more than 70,000 international companies—including banks and trust companies, insurance firms, and mutual funds—having established bases here, it is the fifth largest banking center in the world.[24] The main reason for the Cayman Islands' success is there is no direct taxation of residents or on companies based there. Companies pay only a set fee for a license to operate, certain transactions are kept confidential, and taxes on imported goods are low. In the mid to late 1990s, offshore financial centers like the Cayman Islands came under scrutiny by the Organization for Economic Cooperation and Development (OECD), an organization of 30 countries that oversees and forecasts economic development, for their allegedly harmful tax regimes. The OECD wished to prevent places like the Cayman Islands from having an unfair advantage in the global marketplace and thus being harmful to the economies of more developed countries, so they threatened to place these tax havens on a black list and impose sanctions on them. Such a threat could be disastrous to a small country like the Cayman Islands; however, they managed to avoid being placed on the OECD black list by committing to regulatory reform to improve transparency and agreeing to exchange information with OECD member countries about their citizens.[25]

MINING AND OTHER EXTRACTIVE INDUSTRIES

Mining industries have traditionally been important in certain areas of the Caribbean. In most cases, colonial powers began mining operations, which continued after independence. Jamaica is the world's third-largest producer of bauxite, with the mining operations and the refining companies jointly owned by Jamaica and private companies. Much of its alumina makes its way to the United States. Bauxite is refined and used to make aluminum, a silver-white, lightweight metal that is strong and used in homes and industries. There are many environmental concerns about this critical industry.

Suriname, located on the mainland of South America between Guyana, French Guiana, and Brazil, mines bauxite and gold, refines bauxite into alumina, and exports oil. Multinational corporations mine the bauxite. Many decisions about industrial mining have been taken without consulting indigenous people inhabiting these resource-rich areas. Recently, the government has also started to grant licenses to "informal" small-scale gold miners, many of whom come from Brazil to try to dig a living out of the ground. Some international companies are also interested in taking wood from the tropical forests and in mining diamonds. Much of the interior of the country where these resources are found is inhabited by indigenous communities who are descended from runaway slaves. These areas also are part of an endangered and rare landscape.

CARICOM AND ECONOMIC INTEGRATION IN THE CARIBBEAN: FROM CARIFTA TO CSME

The idea of economic integration in the Caribbean was an attempt to address the problems of these small economies, which are dependent upon a limited number of economic activities. In 1966, after the collapse of the West Indies Federation, CARIFTA was set up as a free-trade arrangement. Leaders had the idea that trade liberalization would help the small Caribbean economies grow and develop. It would create a bigger market for homegrown goods and hopefully encourage more foreign investment who could now count on more customers in a bigger market.

By the 1970s, Caribbean leaders, including then-secretary general William G. Demas, argued that just opening up trade was not enough. They argued that the Caribbean economic area should not only encourage growth through free trade but should also increase local ownership and control of the economy. These

CARIBBEAN BANANAS

George De Freitas works for a company that exports bananas from the Windward Islands as well as being a banana farmer himself.

St. Vincent is completely dependent on bananas. Whereas other crops might only be harvested once or twice a year, bananas give people a weekly income. Farmers do plant other crops but these are usually used as food for the family. There are still some younger people on the farms but lots have left. Farmers paint such a gloomy picture of what it's like that the youth don't want to get involved. We depend heavily on being able to sell at a good price to a good market. If there was a growth in the market for bananas then more people would get involved in production again.

Regina Joseph is a 42-year-old banana farmer from Dominica. She has been involved in banana farming since she was 16. "I spend the whole day on the farm. The farm isn't too far away. Mostly women do the tasks like washing and packing the bananas. Sometimes my daughter helps me pack, but I always do the selection of bananas to sell myself." *

In the Windward Islands—Dominica, Martinique, Saint Lucia, Saint Vincent and the Grenadines, and Grenada—bananas are grown on small family farms, often on hilly terrain. Sometimes the crop is destroyed by hurricanes. Banana farmers often spend ideas led, in 1973, to the creation of CARICOM, which not only removed tariffs between the islands but also involved joint planning for development and functional cooperation.

In the 1980s and 1990s, the CARICOM member economies still seemed trapped by their small size and reliance on a few

more than half their earnings on pesticides, fertilizer, packaging, and transporting their bananas from the farms to the docks. In the late 1990s, as much as 60 percent of export earnings came from the fruit and supported small family banana farms on Dominica, St. Vincent, and St. Lucia.[**] In Ecuador, Mexico, Guatemala, and Honduras, cheaper and more uniform-looking bananas tend to be grown on larger plantations owned by huge multinational corporations. They invest in farming machinery and pay workers little.

Recent changes in world trade rules, including the dismantling of the European Union's preferences for Caribbean bananas, mean small Caribbean farmers now face increased competition from multinational companies, which can grow bananas much more cheaply. In recent years it has become much harder for farmers to earn enough money to support their families. Less income and more poverty, some observers say, are leading to social problems on the islands. Many economists claim that, in the long run, free trade in agricultural and other goods will be the best for everyone, even if in the short run, higher cost producers in small economies like the Windward Islands fail.

[*] Oxfam/Cool Planet, "Banana farming." Available online at *http://www.oxfam.org.uk/coolplanet/kidsweb/banana/farmers.htm*.

[**] Anne Claire Chambron, "Straightening the Bent World of the Banana," February 2000. Available online at *http://www.r0.unctad.org/infocomm/anglais/banana/Doc/banana.rtf*.

industries, including tourism. Many other global regions were creating bigger, regionwide economic spaces. The European Union was becoming an ever-stronger single market, involving the cooperation of many industrialized countries. In the early 1990s, the North American Free Trade Agreement (NAFTA) lowered trade barriers among Mexico, the United States, and Canada. Many Caribbean countries had depended on trade preferences—lower tariffs on their goods than on the same goods from other countries or quotas that favored their products—from larger economies, especially the European Union. But Europe was under pressure to treat Caribbean products like any others, within the framework of the World Trade Organization rules.

In 1989, CARICOM created the Declaration of Grande Anse in Grenada, which established an integrated market and economy, the CSME, while still recognizing the member states as separate political units. They thought that with one economic space, there would be more diverse economic activity and that increased competition in a bigger economy would lead to a higher quality of goods and services available for local consumers and for export. They hoped that such measures would give the Caribbean a stronger position in global economic competition and that more economic activity would lead to higher standards of living and sustained economic development. With the end goal in mind—improving standards of living and work while increasing employment and development—CARICOM decided to commit itself to a single market and single economy in the region.

The CSME was formally established on January 30, 2006, when Barbados, Belize, Guyana, Jamaica, Suriname, and Trinidad and Tobago signed a declaration agreeing to comply with the single market guidelines. The other member states—Antigua and Barbuda, Dominica, Grenada, St. Kitts and Nevis, Saint Lucia, and St. Vincent and the Grenadines joined the single market in June of that year. The establishment and development of this single market and economy is an ongoing project. The heads of government have agreed on 2015 as the goal date for the single economy to be fully operational.

HOW DOES THE CSME WORK?

The CSME is a plan to make a single market and economy out of the small, separate economies of the Caribbean. A unified economy, like that of the United States or any other large country, is held together in many ways. Products and wealth can move around without tariffs or taxes to stop them from going from one corner of the economy to another. Businesses can generally set up in different parts of the economy according to the same basic rules. Workers may move around freely to find work. Products and services need to meet the same standards of safety and quality all across the economy. In general, there is one set of professional qualifications and a standardized educational system that trains people who work in the economy. CSME set out to achieve these sorts of freedoms. The idea was to create a single large economic entity rather than have 15 separate economies governed by its own rules and divided from the others by many barriers.

Free Movement of Goods and Services

Although it was already partly in place, the first objective that the organization sought to fulfill was the free movement of goods and services. At the time of the Grand Anse Declaration, most tariff barriers on goods had already been removed. About 95 percent of manufactured goods—such as specialized filters for industrial uses, steelpan musical drums, shoes, and clothing—now move freely. Still there is work to be done on free movement of services. Insurance companies, banks, architects, and doctors should be free to offer their services across borders. There is already a provision in place to make it easier for businesses originating in one country to freely operate in other countries under the same set of rules. These countries would have to give businesses from any CARICOM country the same access to land, buildings, and other property related to running a business.

Work Permits and Free Movement of People

In a single economy, like the European Union, workers can move freely to look for work. The CSME set a goal to allow skilled and professional workers and those with seasonal or temporary contracts to move freely between Caribbean member states. They also determined that performers, athletes, and journalists should be permitted to travel freely. Later, government leaders decided that a Caribbean national with a university degree could work and live in any member state without a special work permit.

In addition, in order to promote hassle-free movement among the member states, CARICOM issued a common passport. The heads of government believe that it will promote a shared regional identity and decrease discrimination based on nationality. On January 7, 2005, Suriname was the first member state to officially launch the CARICOM passport. Thus far, 11 member states have adopted it.

Free Movement of Capital and Single Currency

The CSME resolved to make it easier for wealth and money to move around within the CARICOM economy. The free movement of wealth allows someone from a member state to invest money in any country within the CSME area in order to develop a business or just to save money. In order for this to happen, the CSME needed to figure out the best way for the many different currencies in use to be exchanged. An exchange rate is the price of one type of money in another, and when these exchange rates are complicated and change often, travel and business become more difficult. The CSME set new rules for exchange rates and also hopes to create a single currency by 2015. They hope that a single currency would provide exchange rate and price stability and reduced transaction costs in regional trade. These benefits would stimulate capital flows and intraregional trade and investment, improve balance of payment performance, and increase growth and employment.

But the single market and economy is not only about freer movement of goods and people. It also reaffirms CARICOM's interest in cooperative planning for development. CARICOM continues to try to encourage entrepreneurs to start businesses and to promote good relationships between workers and employers. It also tries to figure out the best tax policies to encourage economic development. Since agriculture is of major importance on the islands, there is a special agriculture policy that tries to encourage science, technology, and research in agriculture; diversification of agricultural products; and good use of land. Because all modern economies are dependent upon good transportation networks, part of the plan for the single market is efficient transportation systems on land, in the air, and on the sea.

Finally, whenever a bigger, competitive market area is created, some countries—often the already more developed ones—benefit more than others. Some types of businesses die while others flourish, and some groups of people find more job opportunities while others lose jobs that were lifelines not only for themselves but for entire families. The CSME created special programs for some of the least developed countries in the Caribbean and any member state, region, or sector of industry that is especially disadvantaged by the single market. This treaty chapter sets up financial, technical, and economic assistance for areas that are especially disadvantaged.

In July 2007, to show support for the efforts of CSME and to strengthen development of the community, the heads of government reaffirmed the idea that economic growth is a means to the end of better societies over time. They pointed out that in addition to economic growth, CARICOM also aims to create jobs and a good quality of life for all CARICOM citizens, including its young people who often leave the region; social justice and equality; personal security and safety; environmental protection and ecological sustainability; and governments at all levels that are democratic, open and honest, and welcoming to the participation of its citizens.

CARICOM, THE ECONOMIC GIANTS, AND THE WORLD ECONOMY

Upon gaining independence, CARICOM economies were closely tied to European economies. CARICOM countries tried to preserve some of the traditional links and special trading relationships with Great Britain and Europe as well as the United States and Canada. At the same time, the Caribbean countries tried to strengthen the economy of the region and find new trading partners in Latin America and Asia. Over time, world economic organizations have emphasized free trade with no trade preferences between countries. As a result, CARICOM member states have been less able to depend upon special trading arrangements with Europe and the United States.

Still, the United States has maintained a strong link to the Caribbean economy. Since the beginning of the twentieth century, the United States has viewed the Caribbean as its "backyard" and has established various economic initiatives in the region. The United States has created a number of trade laws in partnership with the Caribbean, although they have defined the Caribbean as including not only the members of CARICOM but also Central America.

In 1983, the U.S. Congress passed a program called the Caribbean Basic Initiative (CBI), which was initiated by the Caribbean Basin Economic Recovery Act. Made official on January 1, 1984, it aimed to provide tariff and trade benefits to many Central American and Caribbean countries. There is some evidence that it at least temporarily increased trade in certain commodities, which benefited the Caribbean. In addition, it included some provisions for independent unions and safer workplaces. Yet, in the 1980s, Caribbean leaders who were concerned about growing U.S. protectionism, despite the act, said that the CBI excluded important products including textiles, footwear, and leather products; found that aid levels to CARICOM nations had stagnated; and pointed out that the Eastern Caribbean lacked the necessary infrastructure to take advantage of CBI benefits. Other critics said that it did nothing to address underlying economic and social problems, that its underlying intention was to reward countries siding with the United States in the Cold War, and that it mainly safeguarded markets and sources for cheap labor for U.S. businesses.[26]

NAFTA gave Mexican products preference when imported into the United States, which lessened the positive impacts that the CBI had provided to the Caribbean Basin countries because it increased the import of similar, competing products from Mexico. Still, the United States passed other laws regulating trade with the Caribbean, some of which brought trade with the Caribbean more in line with the terms of trade with Mexico.

In 1974, the European Economic Community, the predecessor of the European Union, set up a specific trade agreement with certain ACP (African, Caribbean, and Pacific) countries. This agreement, which was renewed several times with some modifications, was known as the Lome Convention. It allowed agricultural and mineral exports from ACP countries to enter Europe duty-free. It also gave preferential treatment to products like sugar and beef and pledged $4 billion in aid to these countries.

The European Union, under pressure from the World Trade Organization, banana and sugar producers outside the Caribbean, and businesses of all kinds has decreased the preferential treatment they used to extend to the island economies. In 2000, Europe and 77 developing countries (including those in the Caribbean) signed a new trade agreement. The

Under pressure from the World Trade Organization and organizations outside of the Caribbean, the European Union created a new trade agreement that would reduce preferential treatment for Caribbean-made products. In 2007, hundreds of people protested against economic partnership agreements, saying that the free trade deals proposed by the European Union destroy livelihoods and the environment and undermine future development and regional integration.

long-term plan was to create free trade with no barriers, and in the short term the European Union promised to lower barriers, as did the ACP countries. More recently, the European Union has established economic partnership agreements with CARICOM. These agreements reduce preferences for Caribbean products entering European markets. According to Oxfam, an international organization that supports development in poorer countries, these agreements do not protect and support the Caribbean economies enough. They hand over control of many basic services, such as education, medical services, and sanitation, to private European countries, hindering the ability of Caribbean countries to build up their own structures and abilities, creating the risk that these services will not be available to the poorest members of society.[27]

Some Caribbean leaders have turned their attention to China because of what they feel is flagging interest from the United States and the European Union. China has increased trade with the countries of CARICOM to more than $2 billion in recent years. China uses oil and gas from Trinidad and Tobago and bauxite (aluminum ore) from Jamaica. China's leaders also have designated many Caribbean nations as approved tourist destinations, which are appealing to the growing Chinese middle class. Until recently, the Chinese could travel to countries in the Caribbean only on business trips. It is estimated that by 2020, China will be the world's fourth-largest source of tourists.[28]

CARICOM
Politics

Political independence and democracy are relatively recent developments in the Caribbean. Less than 50 years ago, Jamaica was the first CARICOM country to gain its independence. Yet the Caribbean countries have, on the whole, managed to maintain relatively stable democratic systems. Compared to neighboring Latin America, where there are many countries ruled by dictators and turmoil caused by military coups and civil war, the Caribbean is stable and democratic. Politics within CARICOM member states can be divided into multiparty and two-party systems (Cuba has a one-party system but is not a member of CARICOM). These systems can be traced back to their colonial history.

TWO-PARTY SYSTEMS

Two-party systems can primarily be found in the Anglophone Caribbean, the independent English-speaking countries of the Caribbean that were once colonial territories of Great Britain. Jamaica and Barbados are examples of two-party systems. They are both former British colonies, and both use what could be called the "Westminister model," the British model of parliamentary democracy.

Both have a main, elected lawmaking body and a smaller Senate appointed by political leaders. The party that wins the majority of seats in the parliament, the elected lawmaking body, elects its leader as prime minister, and the prime minister forms the cabinet from his or her party. Because these countries are still in the British Commonwealth, the Queen of England is a ceremonial head of state, but it is the prime minister and cabinet who actually govern. Both countries have independent court systems and a strong rule of law. Neither have political parties at strong odds with each other or with fundamentally different views of the political and economic world.

In some two-party systems, there can be one party that continues to rule instead of alternating the running of the government. For example, in Trinidad and Tobago, the People's National Movement remained in power for 30 years, from 1956–1986. In Antigua, the Antigua Labour Party ruled for more than 40 years, until their defeat in 2004 over corruption charges.

Barbados is also a country with high living standards and a strong democracy based upon British institutions. The country has two main political parties, the Barbados Labour Party (BLP) and the Democratic Labor Party (DLP), which share general positions on politics and economics. In 2008, the BLP, which had been in the majority since 1994, lost the election, winning only 10 seats to the DLP's 20 in the House of Assembly.

Owen Arthur, who had been prime minister since 1994, had to relinquish his leadership position to David Thompson. Some pointed out that the BLP probably lost because they had been in office for a long time, though there were also specific criticisms of the ruling party.[29] Arthur had been a popular leader for his support of continuing the process of making Barbados a fully independent parliamentary republic, replacing the British queen with a Barbadian head of state. During his term he also worked on speeding up the implementation process for the CARICOM Single Market and Economy and supporting the Cricket World Cup in 2007.

MULTIPARTY SYSTEMS

Haiti, Suriname, and Guyana are examples of multiparty systems. These political systems are parties of three or more groups. Seats are awarded according to the number of votes received, so small parties can win seats. This encourages small parties to form and participate in the political system. Suriname has 26 parties; Guyana has 15; and Haiti has 28.

AN IMPOVERISHED COUNTRY WITH AN AUTHORITARIAN TRADITION: THE CASE OF HAITI

Haiti, a former French colony, has a complicated political history. It became the first independent black republic through a combination of an anti-slavery and anti-colonial revolution in the 1790s. Still, the United States did not recognize independent black Haiti for more than half a century. France collected penalty payments for what it said was damage to the property of France and its citizens by the revolution; it also remained hostile.

The new leaders faced a cruel dilemma: Should they allow the former slaves to own and work their own land, or should the new leaders restore a plantation system with a strong army under new ownership and black rule? The new leaders tried to rule with force, many former slaves simply fled, and the economy collapsed. Haiti became a system of a black elite and a mass of poor people trying to survive on small plots of land.

The system of rule almost immediately became an authoritarian one. There had been no hint of representation or democracy under French rule. Poverty remained widespread and acute. Rather than governing in the interests of the society as a whole, fairly and equally represented in an elected parliament, obtaining political power rapidly became one way people could survive—Haitians call it the "politics of the belly." Those holding power have held on by any means necessary. The army, which controls the tools of violence—guns, ammunition, tanks—has been a critical tool for political leaders who want to keep power.

The Duvaliers, father François and son Jean-Claude, ruled from 1957–1986. François, known as Papa Doc, won the 1957 presidential election through a rigged election. Life in Haiti went downhill from there. After exiling the supporters of his opponent in the 1957 elections, Papa Doc created his own special paramilitary forces called the *Tonton Macoutes*. The Macoutes, who were fiercely loyal to Duvalier, had no official salary so they made their living through crime and extortion. In 1961, the United States cut off most of its economic assistance to the country, and in 1964 Papa Doc declared himself president for life. He is estimated to have caused the deaths of more than 30,000 people and exiled thousands more.

In 1971, Jean-Claude, also known as Bébé Doc, assumed the presidency of Haiti at the age of 19 upon the death of his father. Initially, in response to the criticisms and international pressure, Bébé Doc made some effort to do better than his father. He released some political prisoners, eased press censorship, and initiated some judicial reforms. Still, Haiti remained a police state until a popular uprising resulted in his exile in 1986.

In 1990, Jean Bertrand Aristide, a priest who argued that he would stand on the side of the Haitian poor, was elected president. He was overthrown that same year but returned to power

In April 1971, at the age of 19, Jean-Claude Devaulier *(center)* succeeded his father, François, as president of Haiti. Initially, Jean-Claude tried to be a more lenient ruler than his father's regime, but there were no real changes and Haiti remained a police state where the opposition was not tolerated. In 1986, Jean-Claude was forced into exile, leaving behind an economically ravaged country, lacking a functional political foundation and devoid of any practice of peaceful self-rule.

with United States support in 1994. By then, Aristide had abandoned some of his ideas for improving the lives of the Haitian poor, and he used some of the repressive tactics of previous Haitian rulers. Haitian forces, supported by the United States and France, turned against him. In 2000, controversial new elections, in which only about 5 percent of the eligible population voted, resulted in the return of Aristide and his political party, but Haiti continued to lurch from crisis to crisis. In 2004,

Aristide submitted his resignation. An interim or temporary government followed, then new elections in 2006 brought in a new legislature and a new president, Rene Preval.

Haiti's problems are so deep and widespread that most policymakers and social scientists think that only the United States and the United Nations could effectively help rebuild it. The country needs to build personal safety and security, respect human rights while functioning effectively, and have a better functioning economy. Many civil society organizations work in Haiti making great contributions, but the state and society as a whole are troubled. The UN presence has been controversial, with many groups saying they have done little to control the violence of the Haitian police or gangs or to assist in other ways.

CARICOM AND HAITI

In 1997, the Caribbean heads of government agreed to admit Haiti if it met certain requirements, and it was formally admitted to CARICOM in 2002. Its membership was suspended in 2004 following the collapse of the Aristide Party. Caribbean leaders said that Aristide had been unconstitutionally overthrown and that the very basis of democracy had been disregarded. CARICOM leaders were divided. Haiti was re-admitted when new legislative and presidential elections in 2006 came about.

CARICOM has sent official observers to monitor Haitian elections. They wanted to encourage fair elections, but they also used the opportunity to judge whether Haiti was taking steps to democracy and could be admitted to a community that saw itself as democratic. In 2004, one of Haiti's most turbulent years, Caribbean leaders were divided about whether and under what terms Haiti should participate in CARICOM.[30]

Haiti's membership in CARICOM is important for many economic reasons. Several countries in CARICOM have been concerned about illegal Haitian immigrants coming to their shores. For example, the Bahamas needed additional workers but wanted to regulate immigration from Haiti based on law.

Haiti is a potential market with 9 million people, though much of the population is poor. Investment by businesses from other CARICOM countries might help the Haitian economy and consumer, as well as create a larger market for CARICOM goods. CARICOM could take many steps to help a struggling Haiti. It could allow tariff-free access to Haitian goods including agricultural goods, and it could encourage Haiti to increase its own food production and self-reliance by allowing it to have a tariff on rice. There could be joint projects to develop roads and communications in Haiti.

In October 2006, the *Jamaica Gleaner*, a major Caribbean newspaper, had this to say about integrating Haiti into CARICOM:

> The integration of Haiti into CARICOM remains the biggest challenge which the Community has yet to face, owing to the social, linguistic, judicial, political and economic obstacles to overcome. CARICOM's total population is about 14 million, 60 percent of which are Haitian, making the most spoken language in CARICOM not English, not even French, but Haitian Creole. . . . How will we reconcile Haiti's judicial system, which is based on the French Napoleonic Code, with the Caribbean Court of Justice's English common law . . . Haiti has the lowest tariffs in the region . . . Can it join together with CARICOM in its single external tariff? Many quandaries remain to be sorted out. If this integration is achieved, however, it will be . . . a great triumph for the region as a whole."[31]

THE POLICY OF NONINTERVENTION: THE INVASION OF GRENADA

Early in the twentieth century the United States referred to the Caribbean as the "American backyard" and exercised military, political, and economic influence. The Spanish-American War of 1898 detached Cuba from Spain and won the United States the formerly Spanish colonies of the Philippines, Puerto Rico, and Guam. The United States purchased the Danish Virgin Islands in 1917, renaming them the U.S. Virgin Islands. U.S. troops occupied the Dominican Republic from 1916–1924, Haiti from 1913–1934, and Cuba for several years. In 1994 and 2004 the United States sent troops to Haiti to control political violence and prevent a mass exodus of refugees from Haiti to Florida. Puerto Rico remains a U.S. territory, and Cuba is regarded by U.S. governments with hostility. Neither country is in CARICOM.

In an uncharacteristic show of military force in the region, on October 25, 1983, the United States invaded the island of Grenada, a very small state with an area of about 345 square miles and a population of about 103,000. In the 1976 elections, after Grenada won its independence in 1974, the United Labour Party claimed victory, but the opposition, New Jewel Movement, did not accept the result. Street violence began. In 1979, the New Jewel Movement, led by Maurice Bishop, took power and suspended the constitution, aligning itself with Cuba and the Soviet Union. With the Cold War at its peak, U.S. president Ronald Reagan claimed that a runway being built on the island by Canadians, Mexicans, and Cubans was a front for the construction of a Cuban-Soviet airbase. He saw this as a threat to the United States, fearing they would supply Communist rebels in Central America. Meanwhile, in 1983, a breakaway group of the New Jewel Movement seized power and eventually murdered Bishop and others. The Grenada army stepped in to rule.

World opinion was divided. The foreign ministers of CARICOM had been following the instability in Grenada with concern but had reaffirmed the principle of nonintervention. Rashleigh Jackson, the foreign minister of Guyana at the time, remembers that "the Ministers affirmed that the affairs of Grenada were for the people of that country to decide and that, as a result, there should be no outside interference . . . they were of the view that a return to constitutionality was required . . . that the overthrow of a government was contrary to traditional methods of changing governments in the region. . . . They felt it was necessary to hold consultations with the government of Grenada."[32] In 1983, the CARICOM foreign ministers reiterated these points.

Later, the Eastern Caribbean states did join the United States in an invasion. The United States claimed it needed to invade Grenada because it needed to stop the spread of Communism and had to secure the safety of the American citizens studying at Grenada's St. George's University. Nevertheless, the United Kingdom, Trinidad and Tobago, Canada, and the United Nations General Assembly, as well as members of the U.S. Congress criticized the invasion. In fact, the UN condemned the invasion as "a flagrant violation of international law," by a vote of 108 to 9 against, with 27 abstentions.[33] Although the defending forces—made up of about 1,500 Grenadian soldiers and about 700 Cubans, most of whom were construction workers—put up a good fight, they were no match for the naval and air superiority of the invading troops.

October 25 is now a national holiday in Grenada, called Thanksgiving Day, to commemorate the invasion. The country still struggles with the invasion's legacy, particularly the assassination of Bishop and the injustices uncovered within Bishop's regime. There has been some economic development, but widespread poverty remains. Today, Grenada has a constitutional parliamentary democracy. In 2004, after being hurricane-free for nearly 50 years, Grenada was hit directly by Hurricane Ivan. This category 3 hurricane caused an estimated $900 million worth of damage and severely disrupted the agriculture and tourism industries, driving unemployment up to 20 percent. The following year, Grenada was hit again, by Hurricane Emily, causing an additional $110 million worth of damage.[34]

HUMAN RIGHTS

Human rights are rights inherent to all human beings, regardless of nationality, place of residence, sex, national or ethnic origin, color, religion, or language. These human rights are often expressed and guaranteed by treaties and other forms of international law.   International human rights law requires governments to act in certain ways or to refrain from certain acts in order to promote and protect human rights and fundamental freedoms of individuals and groups. Generally recognized rights include civil rights, such as the right to life and to free speech; political rights, such as the right to participate in government and to be treated fairly and equally before the law; and social and economic rights, such as a right to education and the right to work. In addition, international law recognizes certain group rights of self-determination and fair treatment. Avoiding discrimination against individuals or groups and not treating people less fairly because of irrelevant characteristics or their culture is a key principle of human rights law.

The CARICOM countries, once colonies themselves, have consistently supported the right of previously colonized peoples to have independent political systems. They have been active in support of UN actions on behalf of the Palestinians and against the apartheid regime, in which a minority of whites brutally ruled a black majority in South Africa.[35] Still, human rights organizations say that support for individual human rights and certain group rights within the CARICOM countries has sometimes been withheld. The tortured history of Haiti and the political turmoil in Grenada from 1979–1983 violated human rights to life, to fair legal procedures, to free expression and organization. There have been major violations in Guyana. Nonetheless, CARICOM often takes the view that it cannot intervene in the internal politics of its member states, while it tries to move countries toward more democratic constitutions and respect for human rights.

After a rash of killings of lawyers and businessmen in 1974, the Jamaican government granted new, broader law enforcement powers in the Suppression of Crime Act and the Gun Court Act. Together, they allowed the police to disarm entire neighborhoods. The long sentences and lengthy delay in hearing cases of the Gun Court have given rise to constitutional challenges, some which have led to amendments to the Gun Court Act.

Caribbean countries damaged their international reputation on human rights by continuing to support the death penalty, which the populations see as a deterrent to crime. One reason CARICOM has moved toward a Caribbean constitutional court is that the privy council, the previously existing court of appeal, generally questioned the constitutionality of death penalty procedures. In addition, Jamaica and Trinidad and Tobago opted out of the American Convention on Human Rights and the UN International Covenant on Civil and Political Rights in hopes of shortening delays caused by prisoner appeals to international human rights organizations.

Even in the Caribbean countries with relatively stable democracies, there have been issues raised about human rights violations. In the Bahamas, Barbados, Jamaica, and Trinidad and Tobago police and prison guards sometimes commit unlawful killings and abuse prison inmates, according to both the U.S. State Department and many human rights organizations.[36] In Jamaica, which has the largest prison population in the British Caribbean, beatings and abuse of prisoners is reported to be widespread and unpunished. Jamaica is actively training its police force about the limits of police authority, police accountability to the government and public, and appropriate conduct.

In many Caribbean countries, violence against women and abuse of children is reported to be high. Those with HIV/AIDS infections suffer from discrimination and abuse. This, say AIDS workers, only makes the epidemic worse, creating stigma and shame and making both prevention and treatment more difficult.

CARICOM
and the
Environment

THE WORD *CARIBBEAN* BRINGS TO MIND WHITE, SANDY beaches, lush rainforests, and clear seas filled with multicolored fish and coral reefs. Within the Caribbean Basin's nearly 1,600 square miles lies a wide diversity of geographical features. Rocky, craggy coastlines alternate with sandy beaches, while mangrove swamps, lagoons, high cliffs, rainforests, and farmland also are part of the landscape.

Before the arrival of the first Europeans, the indigenous Caribs and Arawaks made limited demands of their environment and feared the uncontrollable forces of nature. European settlers, however, set into motion many transformations of nature as they created transportation routes, cut down forests for massive plantation agriculture, and mined minerals. The advent of the tourist trade in the 1950s again changed the relationship of human activity to the environment. Several countries built ports and tourist facilities, endangering the very features that attracted the lucrative tourist trade.

Within the last 50 years, environmental problems have grown in most countries. In poorer countries, including the Caribbean, there has been an especially sharp edge to the problem of balancing economic and social development with environmental protection. How can these countries develop without damaging their environments? Must economic development sacrifice the environment? Most people realize that continuing to promote development while despoiling the land, air, and water is not responsible behavior. Short-term gain results in long-term disaster. Depleting natural resources creates health hazards and lowers the overall quality of life.

CARICOM has affirmed the importance of developmental growth with environmental protection. Their objective, according to Edward Greene, CARICOM's assistant general secretary of human and social development, is to "integrate the human and social factors of development with the economic and physical elements essential to increasing the well-being and quality of life of the Caribbean peoples."[37] What he means is that it is important, when developing the CARICOM countries by building new airports, hotels, or other tourist amenities, to remember that the economics of such development is as important as maintaining a high quality of life for the people of the islands. Maintaining that high standard of living includes protecting the natural resources that are impacted by the development.

Economists classify environmental problems in poorer, developing countries in two ways. On the one hand, there is the problem of destruction of natural land and marine resources through deforestation, soil erosion, desertification, and other activities. In developing countries, these problems are the result of both corporate development of economic activities valued by governments and populations, or of ordinary people without more environmentally friendly ways of surviving. On the other hand, increasing population and industry creates pollution. Cars, industrial and home wastes, and chemicals used in farming all threaten the environment. Among all the issues facing CARICOM's governors, protecting the environment from both resource destruction and pollution is one of the most important.

The problem in the CARICOM countries and in developing countries in general is not just the lack of government revenue to address these issues. It is also that the poorer parts of the population may be harmed most by environmental problems and by certain environmental measures. If rural sources of water disappear or are polluted, the poor cannot afford to buy bottled water. If large agricultural businesses cut down forests for grazing or crops, the poor may not have access to forest land. Loss of forests leads to soil erosion and, ultimately, extreme weather events, especially droughts, become more intense and have dangerous side effects. Globally, the switch to biofuels, such as ethanol made from corn, has sent the price of food skyrocketing and created a global food crisis. There have been food riots in Haiti, a desperately poor Caribbean country. The poor are also disproportionately harmed by natural disasters, such as hurricanes and floods, some of which are related to climate change. Sometimes the poor contribute to environmental destruction, such as when they cut down trees to make charcoal in order to cook what little food they have.

THE CARIBBEAN SEA

The Caribbean Sea serves many different purposes. It contributes to the economic and social well-being of Caribbean peoples. Tourism and fishing are crucial industries. The sea is one of the world's principal waterways, hosting a large number of ships transporting cargo. In 1983, the United Nations adopted the Cartegena Convention—a set of rules and programs created to protect the Caribbean Sea. Within CARICOM and beyond, there has been concern about the vulnerability of the sea.

Tourism has posed one set of challenges to the sea. The population's desire for development and the interests of corporations in profiting from the region's natural features, combined with lack of public awareness, have damaged coral reefs, marine life, and the coasts themselves. Across the world, population and development tends to cluster on coastlines. Residents and visitors compete for space there. Yet, it is along the coast that some of the richest, most diverse, and most environmentally important ecosystems lie. Although the CARICOM member states have increased awareness of the fragility and importance of these environments, they have only limited resources to monitor sea and coastal life and to enforce rules and regulations.

The shipping of hazardous substances, such as nuclear material and waste, through Caribbean waters is another big threat to the ecology of the sea. The main countries shipping such materials are France, Japan, and the United Kingdom.[38] Other forms of hazardous materials are also of concern and the subject of negotiation between CARICOM and other countries.

WASTE MANAGEMENT

Waste management—treatment and management of all types of waste including industrial, household, sewage, and more—is near the top of the list of environmental issues that the Caribbean is addressing. Migration to the cities, increased tourism, and increased industry have contributed to the increase in waste products and the need to dispose of them in an environmentally friendly way. Improvements in treating solid and liquid waste are hampered by the expense of installing systems to treat it.

The Caribbean Environmental Health Institute (CEHI) was established in 1982 to address environmental health concerns, including the appropriate handling of waste. It provides technical advice to CARICOM's member states. To help in concrete ways, CEHI provides water testing and waste testing

Waste management is a serious environmental issue for the Caribbean Islands, where two important industries, tourism and fisheries, depend on a clean environment. Most developing countries do not have the resources to isolate and dispose of such substances, and many treatment facilities are inadequate. Several Caribbean governments have initiated regulations and secured private donor support for upgrading waste management infrastructure, and sanitary landfills are under development in various island states. Pictured is a landfill in Nevis.

through its lab in St. Lucia. It also currently manages a project to coordinate regional management of biomedical waste, training hospital personnel in how to collect, treat, and dispose of medical waste safely.

NATURAL DISASTERS

Due to location, hurricanes at times batter the region. Almost all member states have been affected by severe storms rated for their intensity in categories of 3, 4, and 5. Some of the most destructive have included Hurricanes Hugo (1989); Andrew (1992); Luis and Marilyn (1995); Georges (1998); Lenny and Floyd (1999); Keith (2000); Ivan and Frances (2004); and Fay, Gustav, Hanna, and Ike (2008). According to USAID, the 2008 Atlantic hurricane season was the third costliest on record, behind only 2004 and 2005, with up to $45 billion in damage. These storms killed 793 people and left hundreds of thousands of people homeless in Cuba, the Dominican Republic, Haiti, and Jamaica.[39]

These dangerous storms kill and injure residents and damage the economy as well as the environment, setting back agriculture and tourism. In 2008, *Coup Magazine* claimed Tropical Storm Gustav alone was to blame for 11 dead and 1,000 left homeless in Jamaica. The damage to the island's road network has been devastating, and repairs were estimated to be around $3 billion. In addition to the human toll, widespread flooding negatively affected banana plantations that had almost been wiped out by Hurricane Dean. This will also affect the country's tourism numbers.[40]

The Caribbean Meteorological Organization coordinates the weather services of all the CARICOM countries and provides general forecasts and guidance. It also provides specialized weather information to key economic sectors, including agriculture, tourism, and aviation. Their services are especially critical during hurricane season, from July to November. In 1991, CARICOM also established a disaster relief response agency, overseen by the heads of government.

Many CARICOM countries are of volcanic origin and several have active or dormant volcanoes. The most active are in Montserrat. La Soufriere in St. Vincent and the Grenadines erupted in 1979 and Kick-'Em-Jenny, off the coast of Grenada, erupted in 1991. In 1995, Montserrat's Langs Soufriere volcano killed 20 people, destroyed the country's capital, Plymouth, villages, livestock, and crops. It forced the evacuation of half

On July 18, 1995, after being dormant since the seventeenth century, the Soufriere-Hills volcano in Montserrat erupted. The eruption, which has been ongoing ever since, caused widespread evacuations and destroyed large parts of the island. Only 4,500 people stayed on the island. Bennette Roach (above) stands in front of the buried courthouse where he once worked.

the population. In 1997, at the 18th Meeting of the Heads of Government of CARICOM, the leaders decided that the Community had a fraternal duty to their fellow member states to help them in their time of need. They pledged cash for the establishment of a CARICOM village of 25 housing units on the north of the island for those residents who remained in Montserrat after the eruption. On December 29, 1999, two years after the devastating disaster, the first phase of the CARICOM village was completed.

WATER AND ENERGY

Fresh water is a limited commodity in most CARICOM countries. The islands have few freshwater lakes and rivers. Rainfall is the main source of fresh water. It is caught in rain barrels and stored in underground cisterns. Some countries desalinate the water, or extract the salt from seawater, to produce drinkable water. During periods of drought, farm animals and crops suffer greatly. According to weather researchers at the University of California-Los Angeles, the Caribbean region has gotten a little less rainfall each year for the past 50 years. Their research indicates that this trend will continue and may even be made worse by global warming.[41]

As both the permanent and visiting populations have grown and as industry has developed, so has the demand for energy in the Caribbean. Most CARICOM member states rely on fossil fuels—coal, oil, gas formed from the organic remains of prehistoric plants and animals—for their energy needs. Trinidad and Tobago and Barbados produce oil and gas; other islands, including Jamaica, Dominica, and St. Vincent and the Grenadines, use geothermal, solar, wind, and wood to meet their requirements.

Many CARICOM countries rely on imported oil and gas. Burning gas and oil creates greenhouse gases—carbon dioxide, ozone, nitrous oxide, and methane—which trap some of the sun's heat close to Earth and warm Earth's atmosphere. Prices of fossil fuels have increased, with no indication that they will go down or stabilize in the foreseeable future; for relatively poor economies, these energy costs are a serious burden. Some member states have begun to use and further develop power from the sun, wind, water, and biofuel—fuel from recently dead plants or certain kinds of wastes—because they do not contribute as much dangerous gases as fossil fuels to global warming and may be cheaper. CARICOM's energy ministry has established the Caribbean Renewable Energy Development Program to encourage and increase the use of renewable energy throughout the region, lessening the dependence on fossil fuels.

CLIMATE CHANGE

Many studies have found that the Caribbean Islands and the 40 million people who live there are on the front lines of vulnerability to climate change, the heating up of the air close to the surface of Earth and the oceans. According to Dr. Carlos Fuller, in the twentieth century, the average temperature in the Caribbean region increased by one degree Celsius and that sea levels are rising two milliliters per year with projections for much steeper rises over the next 40 years.[42] As ocean levels rise, built-up coastal areas in many countries are threatened with flooding, and the smallest low-lying islands could disappear under the waves. This would cause tourism to shrink, agriculture would be threatened, and homes and businesses may be destroyed by rising water and storms. These serious economic consequences will make it much more difficult for the Caribbean countries to reduce poverty, improve the well being of their people, and sustain economic growth. Even though the Caribbean countries have not contributed much to the release of greenhouse gases that trap heat close to Earth's surface, they are likely to suffer.[43]

What can a small and not very powerful region do to stop global warming and its impact? The Belize-based Caribbean Community Climate Change Center (CCCCC) opened in 2005. It tries mainly to anticipate and manage the impact of global warming on the Caribbean. But it also tries to make its voice heard, calling urgently upon more powerful agencies and institutions to slow climate change. It was a strong supporter of the first United Nations Framework Convention on Climate Change in 1992, the first comprehensive effort by the world community to address this issue. Its science advisor, Dr. Neville Trotz, explains: "To adapt, we have to identify more accurately what the risk is, what climate we'll be exposed to in the future."[44] The center monitors changes in the region and uses models to come up with predictions about what will happen in the future. They talk with people working in agriculture, water, and tourism to develop strategies that might protect the region against possible negative effects.

CHALLENGES FROM TOURISM

The tourism industry is a crucial part of the CARICOM economies. Members depend upon it for economic growth and stability, and it is the basis for the livelihood of much of the population. Tourism provides thousands of jobs and generates millions in revenue. According to the World Tourism Council, tourism is responsible for 30 percent of the GDP of the Caribbean region and 25 percent of employment.[45] In some countries, such as the Bahamas, those numbers are much higher.

In 1991, the first meeting of the CARICOM tourist summit took place in Jamaica, The heads of government dedicated funds to support the growth of tourism, agreed to address tourism concerns, and decided to address environmental challenges posed by tourism, especially how to get the public and private sectors to work together to lessen damage caused by tourists.

The natural environment that played such a large role in attracting tourists is now paying a large price for that attraction. The tourism industry has been both a saving grace and a threat to environmental survival. Spilled oil and waste from hotels and other tourist spots has sullied the once pristine waters of the Caribbean Sea and has led to the death of countless reefs and coral beds. Deforestation is a threat to the overall stability of each country. As trees are cut down to make room for luxury hotels and other tourist pursuits, soil erodes, flooding increases, and more pollution is washed into the sea.

If the seas and forests are destroyed, tourists will stop coming to spend money, creating a gap in the region's economy. Supporting and preserving the region's ecology can be costly.

(continues on page 88)

GUYANA AND ITS NATURAL ENVIRONMENT

Guyana, located on the mainland of South America, is bordered by Suriname on the east, Brazil to the south, and Venezuela to the west. One of the smallest countries on the mainland of South America, it is about 83,000 square miles in area. Its estimated 770,000 people have an average per person income of $5,300 per year, at the lower end of the income range of the CARICOM countries.[*] The level of deep poverty is high. Nonetheless, Guyana is one of the most biologically diverse countries in the world. Partly because the early Dutch colonists reclaimed some of the swampy land near the seacoasts for agriculture, 80 percent of Guyana's land is still covered by forest.

Intensive farming—working the soil hard and using many chemicals to fertilize and control pests—has taken a toll on the coastal areas. The widespread use of the chemical DDT (dichlor-diphenyl-trichlorethylene) a few decades ago nearly wiped out certain birds along the coast—the Carrion crow and the chicken hawk. Chemicals also washed into the rivers. In the interior of the country, mining and logging pollute rivers and dislodge native species of animals and plants. The way of life of indigenous people who live in the forests are also often disrupted. In the 1990s, the government allowed more logging firms to harvest the country's hardwood trees. There are recent reports that wildcat gold miners working on a very small scale are undermining the rights of these communities and destroying the environment. "Our observations confirmed that the areas around the mines resemble a moonscape of barren, mounded sand and mud . . . small miners typically wash the topsoil away to get to the gold-bearing clay soil underneath, (so the areas) are infertile and incapable of supporting regenerated rainforest," says Bonnie Docherty, a researcher at Harvard University.[**]

Guyana is taking steps to preserve its diverse environment and the people who live in harmony with it. Control of logging has improved. About 134 different Amerindian communities live in the interior, and about 80 communities have been given legal rights to the land they occupy. They often are involved in planning what will happen to the land. Guyana is also declaring some other parts of the country special conservation areas. Ecotourism is expanding. Ecotourism highlights the natural environment but does so in a way that minimizes the negative impact of visitors on the area.

The tropical Iwokrama forest covers nearly a million acres. Bordered by four rivers, it is home to many large endangered animal species, including the harpy eagle, the jaguar, the arapaima (a South American tropical freshwater fish), the black caiman (a reptile similar to the crocodile), and several hundred species of plants, birds, fish, amphibians, reptiles, and mammals. The Iwokrama International Center for Rainforest Conservation and Development is one of the international leaders in research that has worked closely with local communities to establish and maintain the forest, giving community members a chance to directly assist in its management, and for the community to realize financial benefits. The center promotes ecotourism, education about climate change, conservation, and sustainable forestry by using the forest's natural beauty, modern technology, and the ancient culture and traditional knowledge of the people.

* "Country Profile and Demographics: Per Capita Income," Tong Siak Hen. Available online at http://siakhenn.tripod.com/capita.html; see also CIA-The World Factbook: Guyana. Available online at https://www.cia.gov/library/publications/the-world-factbook/geos/gy.html#People.
** Michael Jones, "Harvard Report Documents Mining Abuses in Guyana," Caribbean Press Releases.com. Available online at http://www.caribbean pressreleases.com/articles/1397/1/Harvard-report-documents-mining-abuses-in-Guyana/Page1.html.

(continued from page 86)

Some CARICOM countries have begun to take concrete action to prevent further environmental degradation by working with conservation groups to preserve the biodiversity of their parks, wetlands, and other fragile areas. In the Dominican Republic, for example, Grupo Jaragua helps to support the Jaragua National Park. The Foundation for the Protection of Marine Biodiversity promotes sustainable use of marine resources in Haiti, and the Bahamas National Trust manages the national park system in that country, which covers 20 percent of its seas.

CARICOM WORKS WITH THE UN

CARICOM nations have not had to tackle the environmental challenges alone. In 1976, the United Nations Environmental Program began to work with CARICOM to develop the Caribbean Environmental Program (CEP), an effort to preserve the region's biodiversity and environmental health in the face of economic development. At the time, municipal, industrial, and agricultural waste had polluted much of the Caribbean, and coastal marine life had been overfished. Farmers and forestry companies had destroyed forests and degraded the soil.

In 1981, 27 Caribbean Basin countries that were involved with the Caribbean Environmental Program adopted the Caribbean Action Plan. They wanted to build regional cooperation around natural resources, strengthen existing institutions, and assist smaller island nations. The plan outlines assistance programs, technical advice, and institutional help available to countries of the Caribbean region. Five years later, CEP enacted regulations that cover oil spills and protect areas, wildlife, and land-based pollution. The CEP's work continues mainly in the areas of environmental education, training, and sharing of information. It has also enacted programs to control polluting run-off into the Caribbean, created guidelines for treating sewage and handling natural emergencies, and developed programs to continue protection of marine and land areas.

CARICOM countries are located in a beautiful but fragile place. CARICOM member states inhabit an environment that is threatened every day by powerful global commercial interests, especially those connected with tourism, environmental developments, such as climate change, that cross regional boundaries, and its own populations as they try to make a living. The organization has worked to prioritize a variety of environmental issues, coming together as a regional group and working with other international organizations. At the World Climate Change Conference, Klaus Toepfer, the Under Secretary-General and Executive Director of the UN Environment Program spoke at the Hague: "We need to start acting now to help those small island nations, least developed countries, and those facing drought, desertification, and other effects of a changing climate system."[46]

Health in
the Caribbean

In 2007, the small Caribbean island nation of Dominica—long ago inhabited by the Arawak and then the Carib peoples on the island on which Columbus alighted in 1493—had 22 adults over the age of 100, more than 3 times the proportion of people over 100 than in richer, developed countries. On October 14, 2003, the person who may have been the world's oldest person, Ma Pampo, died in Dominica. Born in 1875, she had lived on the island for 128 years. She worked much of her life in the sugarcane fields and reportedly rose every morning at five to pray. Ma Pampo was an example of an unusual and not completely understood phenomenon on Dominica—the large percentage of people over the age of 100. The Minister for Health in the island country says, "The whole of Dominica has an environment conducive to long

Hundreds of people wait each day to be seen at clinics in Haiti, the poorest country in the Western Hemisphere. The lack of food, clean water, sewage treatment, and a public health infrastructure has brought on health problems rarely found in developing countries. Above, 600 doctors and medical personnel from a U.S. Navy hospital ship provided free services to Haitian patients in Port-au-Prince.

life. Fresh foods, clean water, pure air, a high level of relaxation, good family support, belief in God, low stress, and lots of exercise —that is what life in Dominica is all about. Our primary health care system is one of the oldest in the region and one of the best or most comprehensive. It is decentralized, and instead of waiting for people to come to us, we take health to them. We reach out to the people."[47] In the Caribbean as a whole there is a trend toward longer life expectancy and an aging population, as well as improvement in many other aspects of health.

Haiti is the exception to this rule. There, men only live an average of 59 years and women 63. Children born in Haiti are more likely to die during early childhood than in any other country in the Western Hemisphere, according to the United Nations Children's Fund (UNICEF). "There are few more challenging places to have a healthy childhood than Haiti," says Adrianao Gonzalez Regueral, UNICEF representative in Haiti.[48] While Haiti has only 2 percent of all the births in Latin America and the Caribbean, it accounts for 19 percent of deaths of children under 5. Children have limited access to shots to prevent diseases like measles, and when they do get sick, they often have to walk for hours to try to reach a health center. Children often do not have sources of clean water or nutritious food. In the cities they are subject to violence and abuse. Children also suffer from AIDS and tuberculosis. Haiti, the poorest country in the Caribbean, is the worst off in terms of health care, not only for children but for the whole population. However, problems of HIV/AIDS, poor nutrition, and violence plague many countries in the Caribbean.

HIV/AIDS

One business that is booming on the small, beautiful island of Tobago is the making of coffins. Emma Joseph, who grew up in Trinidad and is now a journalist in Great Britain, says that people are worrying about what will happen to Tobago's current adult workforce and who will be healthy enough even to have children—who of course are necessary to the future of the island. One young man told her, "I don't know where the next generation will come from. There are only 60,000 of us now, and a lot of people have the disease." One man told her that six friends of his had already died from AIDS. Another told her that one problem was transmission of the disease through incest—sexual relations inside families—and adultery by married men who have sex with younger girls. This combination is disastrous, because if the father catches the virus, he can pass it along to his wife and daughter as well as the girl with whom he commits adultery. "With few proper drugs to treat HIV and AIDS, most are condemned to a very tragic end, and no amount of prayers can save them," she reports.[49]

The second highest rates of HIV/AIDS infection in the world, after sub-Saharan Africa, threatens the Caribbean. At the end of 2001, HIV/AIDS infection rates in the Caribbean were highest in Haiti—about 6 percent of all adults—and lowest in Grenada and Jamaica, and Dominica—just over 1 percent.[50] Overall, health scientists estimate that 2 percent of the adult population through the region carry the AIDS virus.[51]

HIV/AIDS is a fatal, sexually transmitted disease or infection. It can also be spread through exchange of blood products, for example from infected needles that are shared. Once a person has the virus, he or she is infected for life. The virus destroys a person's immune system, making its carriers vulnerable to life-threatening infections like pneumonia and tuberculosis.

In the Caribbean, there are many cases of HIV/AIDS among men who are migrant workers and especially among Haitian men who emigrate out of the desperately poor country of Haiti to work in sugar fields in the Dominican Republic. Many Dominicans found that Haitian migrants were hot spots of the epidemic. A doctor who works with HIV-positive women in a clinic said that the communities of Haitian sugarcane workers were the point of entry for the disease.[52]

Migration within and between countries is only one main factor that seems to push up the number of HIV/AIDS cases. In the Caribbean, poverty sometimes forces women to provide sex for pay. Bad relationships between men and women mean that men do not care if they pass on HIV to their partners. In Haiti, many researchers report, there is a tolerance for violent acts toward women, who may be raped or abused by men with HIV. Throughout the Caribbean, women are over a third of those infected. Sexual activity at a young age increases the risk because young people do not think carefully about the consequences of what they are doing or feel overpowered by older partners and do not take measures to protect themselves from sexually transmitted infection. Substance abuse involves using infected needles and risky sexual behaviors.

In the Caribbean, like other parts of the world, many people do not want to talk about or admit to having AIDS. People are afraid that they will lose jobs, homes, and contact with friends and family if others know they are infected. Only a few health clinics educate people about AIDS or treat those who are sick. Some people are superstitious rather than scientific in their thinking about AIDS; instead of realizing that AIDS is a virus that can be passed from person to person in certain ways, they believe that getting AIDS is a curse or a punishment out of their control.

On the other hand, Caribbean countries have made some progress in limiting the spread of AIDS. National AIDS programs under the leadership of presidents or prime ministers have slowed its spread. In the Dominican Republic, between 1996 and 1999, women who sold sex to men, often referred to as sex workers, became more careful and tried to get male partners to use condoms, which can greatly reduce the probability of HIV transmission during sex. Dominican leaders worked hard on prevention and education. The Nonprofit Center for Human Solidarity and Promotion was one of the country's most successful anti-HIV programs. It found HIV-positive people new work, provided health care, and got sex workers to teach each other and clients about safer sex.[53]

The Pan Caribbean Partnership Against HIV/AIDS (PANCAP) is the regional body that coordinates the Caribbean response to the HIV/AIDS epidemic. Based in the secretariat of CARICOM, it has developed a plan of action with many parts. One part of the plan is to strengthen laws and programs that would limit the spread of AIDS. Another is to find resources to care for people living with HIV/AIDS. In 2002, PANCAP signed an agreement with six large drug companies to provide anti-HIV drugs more cheaply. These drugs have slowed the progress of the virus for many but remain out of reach in many areas of the Caribbean. CARICOM plans to work hard to educate and protect young people and prevent HIV being spread among groups like sex workers.

Mothers can transmit their own HIV infections to newborn babies in two ways—while the baby is still in the uterus or through breast milk. By educating new mothers and making a drug available that can stop babies from being born with their mothers' HIV infections, CARICOM hopes to reduce mother-to-baby transmission of HIV. Other countries, international organizations, and nongovernment organizations are also fighting HIV/AIDS in the Caribbean, and PANCAP tries to coordinate international assistance.[54]

CARICOM has also started a new project to make young people more aware of HIV/AIDS. It includes a public service announcement titled "Get Tested." It encourages everyone to take the blood test for HIV and provides counseling for those whose test results show the presence of the HIV virus. CARICOM has also produced a game show, similar to "Jeopardy." High school students are quizzed on their knowledge of HIV/AIDS subjects including prevention, statistics, stigma, and discrimination.

The United States allocated $16 million from the President's Emergency Fund in 2008 for HIV/AIDS relief for 14 Caribbean countries, and Germany has agreed to donate 8 million euros to HIV/AIDS prevention. Private, nonprofit groups such as Hope for a Healthier Humanity (HHH), founded in New York in 2001, focus on creating educational programs for developing countries in the Caribbean and Latin America. The group offers nursing, medical, and dental students exchange programs and organizes medical volunteers to combat the epidemic. Financial contributions from HHH and many other nonprofit groups help maintain clinics with professional staff, equipment, and medications.

Over 39 million people are infected with HIV/AIDS worldwide. It is a huge problem in the Caribbean, where it has the second highest HIV prevalence rate after sub-Saharan Africa. Domestic and international support for HIV/AIDS prevention efforts have increased, and several countries have established HIV/AIDS commissions.

HIV/AIDS is devastating to families and communities wherever it strikes, but health experts and political leaders have been alarmed by the epidemic in the Caribbean. "The overall threat is very simple; it is affecting the most productive population in the most productive age group," said Patricio Marquez, a health specialist at the World Bank. "There is the risk that an entire generation could be wiped out."[55] It is an especially serious problem in a small region of the world with a limited pool of workers and dependency on tourism.

FIGHTING OTHER INFECTIOUS DISEASES

In the Caribbean, HIV/AIDS remains a threatening infectious disease. Fortunately, many other infectious diseases—diseases resulting from viruses, bacteria, fungi, or parasites passed between people or species—have been conquered or controlled in the Caribbean. Yellow fever, caused by a virus carried by mosquitoes, was brought under control in the early twentieth century. Malaria, a disease caused by parasites carried by mosquitoes, was eradicated in the 1960s. Improved public sanitation and good immunization against diseases played important roles. The Caribbean has eliminated smallpox and polio and was the first region in the world to eliminate some forms of measles. Its immunization rates are extremely high, partly due to the work of the Pan American Health Organization, part of the World Health Organization.[56]

Health leaders in the Caribbean remain vigilant about re-emerging and new infectious diseases, and political and economic leaders worry about these especially because of their possible negative impact on tourism. Even rumors of infectious diseases outbreaks can limit tourist income, and infections can spread quickly in large hotels and on cruise ships. Cholera—of which there were some outbreaks in Guyana, Suriname, and Belize in the early 1990s—and yellow fever—which has not occurred in humans since a 1978–1979 outbreak in Trinidad—are still of some concern. There have been some outbreaks of dengue fever, a mosquito-carried, virus-based disease.[57]

CHRONIC DISEASES

Chronic noncontagious diseases, rather than infectious diseases, are now at the center of health concerns in the Caribbean. Over the last several decades, the main causes of death in the Caribbean have been the same illnesses as in developed countries: heart and circulatory system disease and cancer. Complications from diabetes, a growing problem in the region, also leads to death. As the population of the Caribbean as a whole grows older—fewer young people and more older people as a proportion of the total—chronic diseases like heart disease and diabetes that often begin in middle or old age become more frequent. By 1985, the Caribbean was the area of the developing world with the highest percentage of people aged 55 and over, and by the 1990s life expectancy averaged about 68 years for men and 71 for women.[58] CARICOM points to the fact that obesity—or being extremely overweight—physical inactivity, high cholesterol often linked to poor diet, and smoking lead to preventable chronic illnesses. In 2007, CARICOM declared reducing obesity a major goal. Dr. Fitzroy Henry, the Director of the Caribbean Food and Nutrition Institute, says that obesity "is now the most important underlying cause of death in the region and the range of consequent illnesses is wide among those who survive."[59] Adult women are disproportionately affected; about 25 percent are obese.

CARICOM is also alarmed by a growing incidence of obesity among young children and adolescents. Most public health workers say that obesity is related to poor eating habits and lack of exercise. These, in turn, are related to the way communities are built, with few inviting parks and playgrounds; lots of fast food advertising, even on children's television programs; and high calorie, non-nutritious foods in school lunchrooms combined with reductions in physical education in schools. CARICOM is working for public health messages that emphasize healthy weights. They cite the need for closer regulation and better nutritional labeling of food, especially many high fat foods that are imported. They would like to strengthen the elements of Caribbean agriculture that produce fruits, vegetables, and whole grains. They encourage more gym classes and physical activity in schools.

Falling poverty levels and better scientific understanding have helped limit severe malnutrition due to too few calories or missing nutrients. Still, other nutritional problems have increased. In fact, as countries become richer and import more food, their people's nutrition may get worse in some respects. In the 1960s and 1970s, the economy of Barbados was strong and grew about 4.5 percent a year. In conjuction, the number of food calories available to each person grew, a positive development in stemming hunger. But good carbohydrates, such as whole grains and sugars in fruits, became a less significant part of the diet, and consumption of imported products with animal fats climbed. In Guyana, a country which grew much less during the period, the average calorie intake per person rose only a little bit, but the Guyanese, forced to depend more upon their own agriculture than the Barbadians, moved toward healthier foods—eating less fat and refined sugar. In general, scientists say, food-related and digestive tract-related illnesses are worse in Barbados than in Guyana.[60]

The English-speaking Caribbean exhibits lower rates of tobacco use in smoking and chewing than the rest of Latin or North America. Yet smoking leads to about 10 percent of unnecessary deaths, and the demand for tobacco seems to be growing, not decreasing. In many of these countries, kids experiment with tobacco use when they are between 13 and 18 years old, but many do not smoke regularly or stop altogether. The World Health Organization says that there is a strong feeling in the region, though, that any efforts to limit the sales of tobacco will hurt already fragile economies.[61] It is known that Cuba is a large producer of cigars, but the Dominican Republic and Jamaica also grow high-quality tobacco used in cigars. In some countries, tobacco companies are seen as good partners, even helping to teach school children the dangers of tobacco. In general, governments have been very slow to regulate tobacco companies and sales. CARICOM has recommended raising taxes on tobacco products to discourage people from buying them, labeling tobacco products with health warnings, banning tobacco advertising, and forbidding the sale of tobacco to children.

CARIBBEAN HEALTH SYSTEMS

CARICOM and other organizations agree that a critical measure to improving health in the Caribbean is the strengthening of national health systems. A health system is the total of all the organizations and resources trying to improve health in a country. It includes planners and policymakers, hospitals and clinics; doctors, nurses, engineers, technicians, scientists, and nonprofessional workers who cook and clean in hospitals and clinics; supplies; transportation and communication; and the money that supports all of these activities. A good health system is well planned and organized and affects people's lives every day. It might send a mother a letter explaining that her son is due for an immunization against a deadly illness. It might create a supply of clean water at a village pump, protecting children and adults against waterborne illnesses. It might run programs educating teens and adults about HIV/AIDS, give out medication that helps slow the course of the disease, and care for those with full-blown AIDS. In general, health systems in all countries are overseen by national governments, but exactly what they look like varies a lot.

Many developing countries in the Caribbean and elsewhere, in line with the direction of the World Health Organization, emphasize strengthening "primary health care" or basic, essential health care for all individuals and families in their health care systems. The idea of primary health care is to deliver health services close to where people live and work. It is to serve all people regardless of their income, ethnic group, gender, or urban or rural location at a cost that the country can afford to maintain.

Strengthening the leadership and resources of their health care systems is a primary goal of Caribbean countries. Another major objective is increasing access to health services—especially to the poor. The exodus of doctors from the Caribbean to four wealthy English-speaking countries—the United States, Great Britain, Canada, and Australia—does not strengthen these systems. Jamaica has lost 41 percent of its doctors and Haiti 35 percent.[62] Nurses are also leaving in large numbers to work in wealthier countries.

The Caribbean countries that have increased their spending on education and health care have shown significant progress in productivity and income opportunities. Barbados has ranked consistently in the top 75 countries on the human development index (used to rank countries by level of human development). On the other hand, 40 percent of the population in Haiti has no access to basic health care, only half of the children are vaccinated, and more than half of the population has no access to drugs.

Barbados is one country in the Caribbean with a strong vision of health for its people. The government sees the need to develop a healthy community through a health system that guarantees fair provision of good health care. A healthy population, they believe, will contribute to economic, social, and environmental development. The National Health Policy says health care is a fundamental right of every citizen, and the

Ministry of Health is responsible overall for the health of the population. The Ministry of Health provides a range of hospital services and long-term care for the elderly, and there are also private doctors and clinics and private insurance.

In Haiti, because there has been so much political instability and violence combined with deep poverty, the government has great difficulty in developing a health system. On paper, the Ministry of Health has a hospital in each of nine sections of the country and a health center in every town, but this structure does not really function due to lack of resources. No one

HEALTH AND HEALTH SYSTEMS IN BARBADOS AND HAITI

	BARBADOS	HAITI	U.S.
Life expectancy at birth	72 (male)/ 79 (female)	59/63	75/80
Healthy life expectancy at birth	63 (male) / 68 (female)	43/44	67/71
Infant mortality (deaths of babies under 1 year old per 1,000 live births)	12.8	60	6
Child deaths under the age of five (per 1,000)	12	80	8
Doctors per 10,000 people	12	3	26
Nurses per 10,000 people	37	1	94
Dollars per person spent from all sources on health care per year	1,102	71	6,350

Sources: World Health Organization at http://www.who.int/countries/brb/en/
http://www.who.int/countries/usa/en/; http://www.who.int/countries/hti/en/

knows exactly how many nonprofit and private organizations deliver health services, but they make a great contribution in the absence of a functioning public system. There are terrible health problems, especially in the rural interior of the country.

CAREC, the Caribbean Epidemiology Center, says that not only is there a "natural human quest" for the highest level of health and happiness possible, but that Caribbean leaders are concerned about health because of its impact upon social stability and the economy of the region. Without healthy populations, economies cannot grow and communities cannot thrive. Yet, countries in the Caribbean, like many developing countries, have limited national resources with which to boost their health, and many deeply poor families have no way of obtaining nutritious food or clean water, living in safe communities, or accessing primary health care. For CARICOM, health cooperation within the region and with outside organizations is a critical part of improving the lives of its population.

8

The Future
of CARICOM

As a national of a CARICOM member state, I am yet to be convinced of the effectiveness of this union. Our failure to progress as a strong union is simply because of poor leadership, distrust and short sightedness. The benefits to be derived from a strong and fully functional union is immense, unfortunately our leaders have failed us on the whole regional integration issue. . . . We should learn a few vital lessons from the EU enlargement, the warmness by which the bigger EU states embraced those poor Eastern European states. We all have existing common grounds, such as language, cricket, culture, etc. It's time we stop dithering and put the issue on the front burner and pursue it with vigor and purpose.[63]

—Aleem Hassoo, Guyana

Guyanese citizen Aleem Hassoo, writing to the BBC in July 2008 captures the hopes and problems of CARICOM as an organization. CARICOM originated as a project by Caribbean leaders to create a larger and more effective political and economic entity out of the islands in the Caribbean Basin that once were divided among European colonial powers and shaped to serve their interests. CARICOM's goals have been to strengthen the economy of the region through economic integration and regional economic control and to coordinate regional efforts in education, health, and social welfare. The integration and development project is an attempt to overcome the region's social and economic marginalization in the world, yet in the second half of the first decade of the new millennium, the external environment has grown more challenging.

IS ECONOMIC INTEGRATION POSSIBLE?

CARICOM has taken many steps toward economic integration, yet differences among the Caribbean countries seem to remain a barrier. Some of the more successful countries fear that economic integration—changes in trade, freedom of movement, an attempt to create a common currency—would endanger their fragile prosperity. Many countries seem reluctant to see opportunities for mutual growth through cooperation within the region. Jamaicans have bemoaned the failure of Trinidad to grant lower prices for oil and gas to companies in the region, while several countries have tried to meet their needs both from increased imports of Guyana's rice and with imports from outside the region, which Guyana has opposed.

Many point to the fact that a single economy requires a strong single transportation infrastructure, but regional transportation has been an unresolved issue for decades. "It takes eight hours to get to London from Jamaica. It takes four hours to fly to New York from Jamaica. So then why does it take five hours to get (from Jamaica) to Trinidad, three and a half hours to get to St. Lucia and four hours to fly to Barbados?"[64]

Will CARICOM become a single market and economy by its target date of 2015? And, if so, will this prove to be a key to Caribbean economic development in a competitive global economy?

POLITICAL INTEGRATION

While CARICOM and, before it, the West Indies Federation and CARIFTA have made great strides toward political coop- eration, many people in the Caribbean feel that the leadership of CARICOM itself—the heads of government and the foreign ministers—are simply not willing to take bold steps in CARI- COM and in their own countries to strengthen CARICOM as a decision-making organization.

Norman Girvan, a respected Caribbean scholar and former secretary of the Association of Caribbean States, argues that it is time to transfer real decision-making power to CARICOM itself. Girvan says, "We're still clinging to the insular sover- eignty that. . . is largely fictitious because in the modern world states of our size simply cannot expect to have any real sover- eignty. The forces of globalization, the fact of our small size, the fact of our trade dependency, the fact of our military weak- ness, all of these things make it virtually impossible for our small island states to have any real sovereignty."[65] CARICOM remains a group of states that jealously guard their powers to make the rules for their own territories; CARICOM is not yet a group that can make decisions that are binding on all countries in the group.

CARICOM remains quite different from the European Union. Europe has a powerful commission that works to advance the integration of Europe, proposing many new inte- gration projects and taking considerable responsibility for the single market. CARICOM has no strong commission. In addi- tion, certain laws and policies passed by the institutions of the

CARICOM has taken major steps to be able to compete effectively in the international marketplace. Building relationships with countries like the United States, Canada, and Spain are crucial to ensuring their survival in a rapidly changing global environment. In 2006, at the 3rd CARICOM-Spain Summit, Spain offered assistance in establishing the Regional Development Fund, a key element of CSME.

European Union—its Council of Ministers and its parliament—are binding to the member states. Some advocates of Caribbean integration recommend a Single CARICOM Act that would allow CARICOM decisions to become law and policy automatically in the countries of the community.

CURRENT GLOBAL PRESSURES

The global environment is very challenging, creating different urgent concerns in the member states but also suggesting to many a greater need than ever for integration and joint action. The new Economic Partnership Agreements with the European Union are both very important and very controversial in the

region. Guyana has said it would not sign the agreement nego-
tiated by a wider Caribbean forum with the European Union.
Representatives of workers in the region are also opposed.
Globally rising oil and food prices are of great concern to
the CARICOM states. It is not only the public, official world
economy, but also the illegal global drug trade that threatens
the Caribbean. As a result of their geographic location, many
nations of the Caribbean are used as transit countries to shift
cocaine, marijuana, and other illicit drugs from South America
to the United States, Europe, and elsewhere. Rising global
temperatures also create serious problems for the Caribbean,
dependent upon the seas around them and vulnerable to
extreme weather, creating great incentives for Caribbean cooperation in global discussions about climate change.

ONE CULTURE?

The cultures of the Caribbean Islands and continent countries are unique but enjoy some commonalities. The islands
are marked by their individual histories: they had different
colonizers, host different ethnic and language groups, and
experienced different economic and political histories. At the
same time, Caribbean cultures are all shaped by colonialism,
historically implanted populations and ethnic diversity, the
impact of Caribbean geography, European languages modi-
fied by African and Asian influences, Christianity and other
religious practices, and a unique arts and festival culture.

CARICOM recognizes and supports this rich and evolving
culture. CARICOM supports this Caribbean culture, primarily by its close association with and support of CARIFESTA,
the Caribbean Festival of the Arts. CARICOM's current
secretary general, Edwin Carrington, has pointed to "common culture" as a factor underlying the possibility of a single
market and economy, asserting that "the foundation of our
regionalism is located in the common historical and cultural
heritage of the Caribbean."[66]

The Honorable P.J. Patterson, prime minister of Jamaica, in a November 2004 speech, discussed the cultural commonalities which some think will re-energize economic and political integration:

> We are a chain of islands and sub-continental landscapes woven into a quilt of shared geographic space, and endowed with a unique texture of a unique Caribbean blend fomented by our achievements and aspirations, which are the same from Suriname in the south to the Bahamas in the north. From Belize to Barbados, the region flows with our people's blood, sweat and tears. . . . We must advance and nurture our collective identity through deeper, more profound integration. We have nothing to lose and everything to gain from strengthening understanding, identity and contact between our people as we advance CARICOM integration.[67]

The ultimate question becomes: Will people in the Caribbean think of themselves as Caribbean rather than as Jamaican or Trinidadian or Guyanese, and can this "collective identity" advance economic and political integration?

CHRONOLOGY

1958–1962	Federation of the West Indies is established on January 3, 1958, but collapses four years later due to internal political conflicts.
1965	Antigua, Barbados, and Guyana sign the Agreement of Dickenson Bay, establishing CARIFTA in Antigua.
1969	The Caribbean Development Bank, headquartered in Bridgetown, Barbados, is founded on October 18.
1973	In Chaguaramas, Trinidad, the Treaty of Chaguaramas establishes the Caribbean Community and Common Market (CARICOM).
1989	CARICOM Heads of Government create the CARICOM Single Market and Economy (CSME).
1992	The West Indian Commission publishes its final report called Time for Action. It outlines initiatives to achieve CARICOM's goal of becoming a more closely integrated community of sovereign states.
1993	The CARICOM Youth Ambassador Program (CYAP) is launched as part of the twentieth anniversary celebrations of the Treaty of Chaguaramas.
	Suriname joins as the fourteenth member of CARICOM.
1997	Caribbean-United States Summit held in Bridgetown, Barbados, in order to strengthen ties between the United States and CARICOM.
	Haiti begins process of joining CARICOM. Becomes provisional member in 1998.
1981	The Treaty of Basseterre establishes the Organization of Eastern Caribbean States (OECS).
2001	Revised Treaty of Chaguaramas establishes the Caribbean Community, including the CARICOM

Single Market Economy. All member states sign except the Bahamas and Montserrat.

2002   Haiti becomes full member of CARICOM.

2004   CARICOM suspends Haiti's membership after Gérard Latortue is appointed prime minister of Haiti, following the ouster of Jean-Bertrand Aristide.

2005   The Caribbean Court of Justice (CCJ) is inaugurated in Port of Spain, the capital of Trinidad and Tobago.

Suriname becomes the first member state to issue the CARICOM passport.

Thirteen of fifteen CARICOM countries sign the Petrocaribe, an oil alliance with Venezuela permitting them to purchase oil on conditions of preferential payment.

2006   Suspension of membership is lifted for Haiti. They are readmitted in August.

2007   International Cricket Council (ICC) celebrate the Cricket World Cup in nine member countries in the Caribbean Community.

2008   The European Union and 13 Caribbean countries sign the CARIFORUM-EU Economic Partnership Agreement (EPA). The EPA is intended to strengthen North-South trade, development, and regional integration in the Caribbean.

NOTES

Chapter 1

1. "From High Seas to High Life," Caribbean-Guide.info. Available online at *http://caribbean-guide.info/past.and. present/history/*.

2. "Abolition of Slavery in the Americas," National Museums Liverpool-International Slavery Museum. Available online at *http://www.liverpoolmuseums.org.uk/ism/slavery/ americas/abolition_americas.aspx*.

3. Harcourt Education. *Encyclopedia of the Middle Passage 2007*. New York: Greenwood Publishing Group, xix.

4. "Slave Routes," Breaking the Silence: Learning about the Transatlantic Slave Trade-Netherlands. Available online at *http://www.antislavery.org/breakingthesilence/slave_routes/ slave_routes_netherlands.shtml*.

5. Nicholas Canny, *The Origins of Empire, The Oxford History of the British Empire Volume 1*. New York: Oxford University Press.

6. "Moyne Papers on West India Commission, 1938–1939." Available online at *http://www.casbah.ac.uk/cats/archive/ 135/ICSA00019.htm*; see also Richard Hart, "Labour Rebellions of the 1930s in the British Caribbean Region Colonies," Libcom.org. Available online at *http://libcom. org/library/labour-rebellions-1930s-british-caribbean-region- colonies-richard-hart*.

7. "Caribbean Small States—Growth Diagnostics," World Bank. Available online at *http://siteresources.worldbank.org/ INTDEBTDEPT/Resources/4689801206974166266/48339 16-1206989877225/KidaSmallStates.pdf*.

8. Ibid.

Chapter 2

9. "UWI Mission Statement," The University of the West Indies. Available online at *http://www.open.uwi.edu/about uwi/mission.php*.

10. Dr. Eric Williams quoted in "Trinidad and Tobago, Grenada, St. Lucia, St. Vincent and the Grenadines Sign Memorandum of Understanding." Available online at *http://news.bn.gs/article.php?story=20080826003453808& mode=print.*

11. "H.E. President Bharrat Jagdaeo's CARICOM Day Message," *Guyana Chronicle.* Available online at *http://www. guyanachronicle.com/ARCHIVES/archive%2007-07-08. html.*

Chapter 3

12. "Mr. Edwin Carrington Secretary-General Caricom (1992-present)," CARICOM Secretariat. Available online at *http://www.caricom.org/jsp/projects/personalities/edwin_ carrington.jsp?menu=projects.*

13. "About the Caribbean Court of Justice." The Caribbean Community. Available online at *http://www.caribbeancourt ofjustice.org/about3.htm.*

14. Yasmin Morais, "The Caribbean Court of Justice: A Research Guide" February 27, 2008. Available online at *http:// www.llrx.com/features/caribbeancourtofjustice.htm*; See also "Caribbean Court of Justice Becomes Guyana's Final Court of Appeal," November 6, 2004. Available online at *http:// www.ttgapers.com/Article1072.html.*

Chapter 4

15. "Effects on Bahamas Tourism," Report by The Caribbean Hotel Association. Available online at *http://www. usatoday.com/weather/hurricane/1999/atlantic/wftbaham.htm.*

16. "Facts About the Cayman Islands," World Facts Index. Available online at *http://worldfacts.us/Cayman-Islands. htm.*

17.   George Gmelch, *Behind the Smile: The Working Lives of Caribbean Tourism*, Bloomington: Indiana University Press, 2003.

18.   Carol Horne, "Protecting Views: The Role of Land Trusts in Island Landscape Preservation," Available online at *http://www.landtrust.ca/carolpaper*.

19.   Bert Wilkinson, "Caribbean: Mega-farms Could Ease Food Import Bill," IPS-Inter Press Service. Available online at *http://ipsnews.net/news.asp?idnews=42600*.

20.   Lauretta Burke and Jonathan Maidens, "Reefs at Risk in the Caribbean," World Resources Institute-*Earth Trends*. Available online at *http://earthtrends.wri.org/features/view_feature.php?fid=55&theme=1*.

21.   Donna Spencer and Herold Gopaul, "Climate Change—One More Assault on Fisheries," *IWCAM Caribbean Waterways*, Volume 2 Issue 2, June 2008. Available online at *http://www.iwlearn.net/iw-projects/Fsp_112799467151/newsletters/iwcam-june-2008-newsletter*.

22.   Burke and Maidens, "Reefs at Risk in the Caribbean."

23.   "Bermuda—History and Heritage," Smithsonian.com, November 6, 2007. Available online at *http://www.smith-sonianmag.com/travel/destination-hunter/bermuda-history-heritage.html*.

24.   "Places in the Sun," *The Economist*, no. 382, 3-5.

25.   Natasha Lance Rogoff, "Haven or Havoc?" *PBS Frontline*. Available online at *http://www.pbs.org/wgbh/pages/frontline/shows/tax/schemes/cayman.html*.

26.   "Seventh Report to Congress on the Operation of the Caribbean Basin Economic Recovery Act," Office of the United States Trade Representative, December 31, 2007. Available online at *http://www.ustr.gov/assets/Trade_Development/Preference_Programs/CBI/asset_upload_file373_13752.pdf*; see also Andres Serbin, "The Caribbean: Myths and Realities for the 1990s," *Journal of Interamerican*

Studies and World Affairs, Vol. 32, No. 2 (Summer 1990) 121-141; Addington Coppin, "Trade and Investment in the Caribbean Basin Since the CBI" *Social and Economic Studies* 41:1 (1992) 21-43).

27. "Partnership or Power Play?" Oxfam. Available online at *http://www.oxfam.org.uk/resources/policy/trade/downloads/ bp110_epas.pdf*.

28. Linda Straker, "Caribbean Tourism to Benefit from Historic Agreement Between China and U.S.," *Global Travel Industry News*. Available online at *http://www.eturbonews. com/417/caribbean-tourism-benefit-historic-agreement- between-china-and-us*.

Chapter 5

29. "Thompson Sworn in as Barbados PM," *China View*. Available online at *http://news.xinhuanet.com/english/2008-01/ 17/content_7440232.htm*.

30. "Caricom Observers for Haiti Elections," CARICOM. Available online at *http://www.caricom.org/jsp/pressreleases/ pres27_06.jsp*.

31. Myrtha Desulme, "Caricom and Haiti: The Raising of the Caribbean's 'Iron Curtain,'" *Jamaica Gleaner*. Available online at *http://www.jamaica-gleaner.com/gleaner/2006 1008/focus/focus5.html*.

32. Rashleigh Jackson, "Non-intervention and Intervention: CARICOM in Action - Grenada 1979 and 1983," Guyana- CaribbeanPolitics.com. Available online at *http://www. guyanacaribbeanpolitics.com/guyanafeatures/jackson.html*.

33. "Assembly Calls for Cessation of 'Armed Intervention of Grenada,'" *UN Chronicle*. Available online at *http://find articles.com/p/articles/mi_m1309/is_v21/ai_3073305*.

34. Kari Coley, "Grenada Rebuilds After the Hurricane," *UN Chronicle Online Edition*. Available online at *http://www. un.org/Pubs/chronicle/2005/issue3/0305p07.html*.

35.   Jacqueline Anne Braveboy-Wagner, "The English-Speaking Caribbean States: A Triad of Foreign Policies" in Jeanne A. K. Hey, ed., *Small States in World Politics: Explaining Foreign Policy Behavior.* Boulder: Lynne Rienner Publishers, 2003, 41.

36.   "U.S. Paints Bleak Picture of Human Rights Violations in the Caribbean," *Caribbean Today.* Available online at *http://www.caribbeantoday.com*; see also "Unacceptably Limiting Human Rights Protection," Amnesty International. Available online at *http://asiapacific.amnesty.org/library/Index/ENGAMR050011999?open&of=ENG-GUY*; Stephanie Vascianne, "Caribbean Human Rights: Are We Below Average?" *The World Today.* Available online at *http://sta.uwi.edu/iir/news/theworldtoday/article23.pdf*.

Chapter 6

37.   "Opening Address by Dr. Edward Greene, Assistant Secretary-General, Caricom, at the Thirteenth Meeting of the Council for Human and Social Development (COHSOD), October 26, 2005, Georgetown, Guyana," CARICOM Secretariat. Available online at *http://www.caricom.org/jsp/pressreleases/pres177_05.jsp*.

38.   "Transhipment of Nuclear Waste: Is It Safe?" United States Environmental Protection Agency-Caribbean Currents, Volume 7, Number 3, July 1999.

39.   "Latin America and the Caribbean-Hurricane Season 2008," USAID. Available online at *http://www.usaid.gov/our_work/humanitarian_assistance/disaster_assistance/countries/lac/template/fs_sr/fy2008/lac_hs_fs03_09-10-2008.pdf*.

40.   "Hurricane Damage: Can the Caribbean Economies Keep Bouncing Back?" *The Coup* Magazine. Available online at *http://thecoupmagazine.blogspot.com/2008/09/hurricane-damage-can-caribbean.html*.

41. Stuart Wolpert, "Parts of Caribbean and Central America Likely to Have Less Summer Rain, Computer Climate Simulations Agree, UCLA Atmospheric Scientists Report," UCLA Newsroom. Available online at *http://newsroom. ucla.edu/portal/ucla/Parts-of-Caribbean-and-Central-6972. aspx?RelNum=6972.*

42. "Climate Change in Caribbean Demands Urgent Mitigation, Says OAS Seminar," Caribbean Net News.com. Available online at *http://www.caribbeannetnews.com/ cgi-script/csArticles/articles/000052/005251.htm.*

43. "Economic Impact of Climate Change under Review," Caribbean360.com. Available online at *http://www. caribbean360.com/News/Caribbean/Stories/2008/09/15/ NEWS0000006319.html*; see also "Caribbean faces stormier future" BBC News. Available online at *http:// 2006/08/28 http://news.bbc.co.uk/go/pr/fr-/-/2/hi/science/ nature/5290818.*

44. "Climate Change in Caribbean Demands Urgent Mitigation and Adaptation," Organization of American States.

45. H. E. Carlston Boucher, "No Island Is an Island," United Nations Environment Program. Available online at *http:// www.unep.org/OurPlanet/imgversn/101/boucher.html.*

46. "UNEP Speaks for the Poor and the Environment," United Nations Environment Program. Available online at *http:// www.unep.org/Documents.Multilingual/Default.asp?Docum entID=180&ArticleID=2700&l=en.*

Chapter 7

47. Tony Deyal, "Living to 100," *Perspectives in Health Magazine.* Available online at *http://www.paho.org/English/DPI/ Number15_article1_5.htm.*

48. "Survival Is Greatest Challenge for Haiti's Children," UNICEF. Available online at *http://www.unicef.org/ media/media_31793.html.*

49. Emma Joseph, "AIDS Threatens Caribbean Paradise" BBC News, 25 June 2002. Available online at *http://news.bbc.co.uk/2/hi/programmes/from_our_own_correspondent/2057943.htm.*

50. Bilali Camara, "20 Years of the HIV/AIDS Epidemic in the Caribbean: A Summary," Pan American Health Organization. Available online at *http://www.carec.org/pdf/20-years-aids-caribbean.pdf.*

51. Human Development Sector Management Unit, Latin America and the Caribbean Region, World Bank. "HIV/AIDS in the Caribbean: Issues and Options" Report No. 20491-LAC. June 2000. Available online at *www.un.org/works/goingon/HIV/AIDSCaribbean.pdf.*

52. David Gonzales, "As AIDS Ravages Caribbean, Governments Confront Denial," New York Times, May 18, 2003. Available online at *http://query.nytimes.com/gst/fullpage.html?res=9903EEDE123EF93BA25756C0A9659C8B63.*

53. Ibid.

54. "PANCAP," CARICOM. Available online at *http://www.caricom.org/jsp/projects/pancap.jsp?menu=projects.*

55. Gonzales, *New York Times.*

56. Knox Hagley, "Nutrition and Health in the Developing World: the Caribbean Experience." *Proceedings of the Nutrition Society* (1993) 52, 183-7.

57. Dr. C. James Hospedales, "Overview of Health in the Region," Caribbean Epidemiology Center. Available online at *http://www.carec.org/overview_health.htm.*

58. Hagley, *Proceedings of the Nutrition Society.*

59. Fitzroy Henry, "New Strategies Needed to Fight Obesity in the Caribbean," and "The Obesity Epidemic: The Case for Public Policies," *Cajanus,* Vol. 37, No. 1, 2004. Available online at *http://www.Amro.who.int/English/CFNI/cfni-caj37No104.htm.*

60. Hagley.

61. Heather Selin, Jaime Perez Martin, and Armondao Peruga, "Regional Summary for the Region of the Americas," PAHO. Available online at *http://www.cancer.org/down loads/TOB/PAHO_Summary.pdf.*

62. Celia Dugger, "Devastating Exodus of Doctors from Africa and the Caribbean Is Found," *New York Times*, October 27 2005.

Chapter 8

63. "What Future for Caricom?" BBCCaribbean.com. Available online at *http://www.bbc.co.uk/caribbean/news/story/ 2008/06/080627_havesaycaricom.shtml.*

64. "What Good Is Caricom? Regional Unity Losing Steam," *Jamaica Observer*, July 4, 2008. Available online at *www. bilaterals.org/article-print.php3?id_article=12614.*

65. Ibid.

66. "Respect All Cultures, Says CARICOM Secretary-General," CARICOM Secretariat. Available online at *http://www. caricom.org/jsp/pressreleases/pres145_08.jsp.*

67. Speech by the Most Hon. P. J. Patterson On, PC, QC, MP, Prime Minister, Jamaica at the Launch of the Publication, CARICOM: Our Caribbean Community-An Introduction," CARICOM. Available online at *http://www.jis.gov.jm/ special_sections/CARICOMNew/speechByPatterson.html.*

BIBLIOGRAPHY

Camara, Bilali, "20 Years of the HIV/AIDS Epidemic in the Caribbean: A Summary." Available online. URL: http://www.carec.org/pdf/20-years-aids-caribbean.pdf.

Caribbean Epidemology Center (CAREC). "Overview of Health in the Region." Available online. URL: http://www.carec.org/overview_health.htm.

CARICOM. "Caribbean Unity to Fight Chronic Diseases Epidemic: Obesity A Major Target." August 28, 2007.

———. "PANCAP" Available online. URL: http://www.caricom.org/jsp/projects/pancap.jsp?menu=projects.

Deyal, Tony. "Living to 100." *Perspectives in Health Magazine*, Vol. 7, Nov. 3, 2002. Available online. URL: http://www.paho.org/English/DPI/Number15_article1_5.htm.

Dugger, Celia. "Devastating Exodus of Doctors from Africa and Caribbean Is Found." *New York Times*. October 27, 2005. Available online. URL: http://www.nytimes.com and http://www.culturaleconmics.atfreeweb.com.

Gonzales, David. "As AIDS Ravages Caribbean, Governments Confront Denial." *New York Times*, May 18, 2003. Available online. URL: http://www.nytimes.com.

Hagley, Knox. "Nutrition and Health in the Developing World: the Caribbean Experience." *Proceedings of the Nutrition Society* (1993) 52, 183-7.

Henry, Fitzroy, "New Strategies Needed to Fight Obesity in the Caribbean," see also "The Obesity Epidemic: The Case for Public Policies." *Cajanus*. Vol. 37, No. 1, 2004. Available online. URL: www.amro.who.int/English/CFNI/cfni-caj37No104.htm.

Human Development Sector Management Unit, Latin America and the Caribbean Region, World Bank. "HIV/AIDS in the Caribbean: Issues and Options." Report No. 20491-LAC. June 2000. Available online. URL: www.un.org/works/goingon/HIV/AIDSCaribbean.pdf.

Joseph, Emma. "AIDS Threatens Caribbean paradise." BBC News, June 25, 2002. Available online. URL: http://news. bbc.co.uk/2/hi/programmes/from_our_own_correspondent/ 2057943.htm.

Selin, Heather, Jaime Perez Martin, and Armondao Peruga. "Regional Summary for the Region of the Americas." Available online. URL: http://www.cancer.org/downloads/TOB/ PAHO_Summary.pdf.

UNICEF. "Survival is Greatest Challenge for Haiti's Children." Available online. URL: http://www.unicef.org/media/media_ 31793.html.

World Health Organization, "Barbados." Available online. URL: http://www.who.int/countries/brb/en/.

———, "Haiti." Available online. URL: http://www.who.int/ countries/hti/en/.

———, "United States." Available online. URL: http://www. who.int/countries/usa/en/.

FURTHER READING

Braveboy-Wagner, Jacqueline Anne. *Small States in Global Affairs: The Foreign Policies of the Caribbean Community.* New York: Palgrave Macmillan, 2007.

CARICOM Secretariat. *CARICOM: Our Caribbean Community—An Introduction.* Ian Randle Publishers, 2005.

Cross, Malcolm. *Urbanization and Urban Growth in the Caribbean.* New York: Cambridge University Press, 1979.

De Kadt, Emanuel. *Patterns of Foreign Influence in the Caribbean.* New York: Oxford University Press, 1972.

Dubois, Laurent. *A Colony of Citizens: Revolution and Slave Emancipation in the French Caribbean, 1787-1804.* University of North Carolina Press, 2006.

Hall, Kenneth and Myrtle Chuck A. Sang, eds. *Intervention Border and Maritime Issues in CARICOM.* Ian Randle Publishers, 2007.

Hart, Richard. *Time for a Change: Constitutional, Political, and Labour Developments in Jamaica and Other Colonies in the Caribbean Region, 1944-1955.* Arawak Publications, 2004.

WEB SITES

Caribbean Islands: A Country Study
http://countrystudies.us/caribbean-islands/

Caribbean Newspapers.com
http://www.caribbeannewspapers.com/

CARICOM
http://caricom.org/

Caribbean Festival of the Arts (CARIFESTA)
http://www.carifesta.net/x/home.php

Digital Library of the Caribbean
http://www.dloc.com/

PICTURE CREDITS

INDEX

BRENDA LANGE has been a writer and editor for more than 20 years. During that time, she has written for newspapers, magazines, trade publications, and a wide variety of business clientele. *CARICOM* is her seventh book for Chelsea House. She also has revised two other titles. Lange is a member of the American Society of Journalists and Authors (ASJA) and the Society of Professional Journalists (SPJ). She lives and works in Doylestown, Pennsylvania. Feel free to contact Ms. Lange at www.brendalange.com.

Series editor **PEGGY KAHN** is a professor of political science at the University of Michigan-Flint, where she teaches world and European politics. She has been a social studies volunteer in the Ann Arbor, Michigan, public schools, and she helps prepare college students to become teachers. She has a Ph.D. in political science from the University of California-Berkeley and a B.A. in history and government from Oberlin College. She has lived in Europe and visited South Africa.